TEA SHOP WALKS
IN
SHROPSHIRE

Julie Meech

Published by Sigma Leisure – an imprint of Sigma Press, 1 South Oak Lane, Wilmslow, Cheshire SK9 6AR, England.

British Library Cataloguing in Publication Data
A CIP record for this book is available from the British Library.

ISBN: 1-85058-598-9

Typesetting and Design by: Sigma Press, Wilmslow, Cheshire.

Cover: Stokesay Castle, near Craven Arms *(the author)*

Maps: Jeremy Semmens

Photographs: the author

Printed by: MFP Design & Print

Dedicated to:
Jo and Simon, with love

Acknowledgements:
Thanks to Terry for help and advice, above all for so selflessly sharing the task of checking out all those tea shops, and for allowing me to introduce him to the joys of public transport in Shropshire!

This book has been compiled in accordance with the Guidelines for Writers of Path Guides published by the Outdoor Writers' Guild.

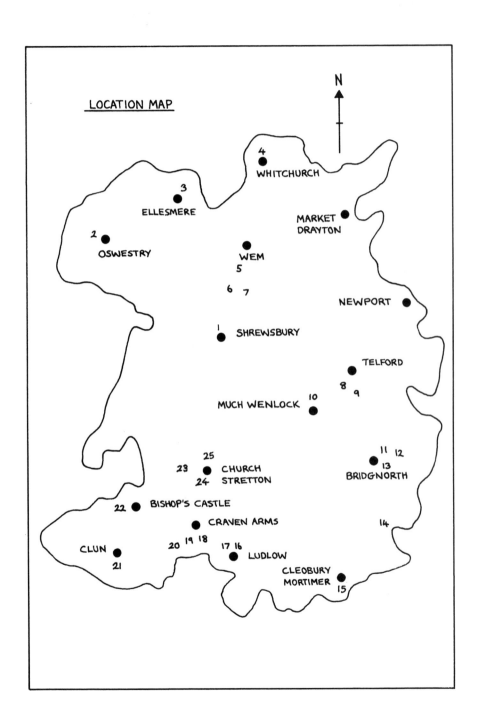

LOCATION MAP

Contents

The Walks

An Introduction to Shropshire

Choose a clear day and take the well-trodden path which leads to the top of the Wrekin, just a few miles from the sprawling new town of Telford. The Wrekin is not Shropshire's highest hill, nor its most scenic, but that doesn't matter for it is more than just a hill. It's the spiritual heart of Shropshire, the embodiment of home to all true Salopians – sentiments reflected in the traditional toast "To all friends round the Wrekin".

A plug of volcanic rock nearly a thousand million years old, the Wrekin stands in splendid isolation, seeming higher than its modest 1334ft (407m). From the top you can look down on one of England's largest counties, that "land of lost content" so wistfully evoked in the poetry of A.E. Housman. With the aid of a map and binoculars you can trace the course of Britain's longest river as the Severn sweeps through Shropshire, forsaking Powys below the Breidden Hills in the west, looping round Shrewsbury, surging through Ironbridge Gorge and finally slipping smoothly through the "wild green hills of Wyre" into Worcestershire

What is most obvious about the river as seen from the Wrekin is how it marks the boundary between the two Shropshires: the uplands and the plain. To the north is a level patchwork of fields, copses, meres and mosses merging seamlessly into Cheshire, and broken only occasionally by modest hills, of which the Wrekin itself is the most commanding. This northern area has its highlights, notably places such as Nesscliffe and Grinshill, battered ridges of red sandstone held in the grip of gnarled Scots pines whose roots search out and cling to every crevice to anchor themselves securely to the craggy tops. Then there are the silver-smooth meres, serenely beautiful in early morning mist, occupying the hollows left in glacial moraine by the retreating ice sheet around 10 000 years ago. More exciting, perhaps, is the north-west corner near Oswestry, where the unruly Welsh hills come tumbling onto the plain and Offa's Dyke marks the ancient demarcation between Saxon and Celt.

Also at Oswestry is Hên Dinas, a 2,500 year-old hillfort which is one of the finest in Britain. Its huge size offers ample scope for exploration and its elaborate system of banks and ditches can't fail to impress. Such Iron Age hillforts are a major feature of the Shropshire landscape. The one whose ramparts encircle the top of the Wrekin is thought to have been the headquarters of the Cornovii, who flourished before the Roman invasion. But the same is sometimes claimed of the fort on Caer Caradoc, highest of the shapely Stretton Hills which catch your eye as you gaze south of Severn at the 300 square miles of the Shropshire Hills Area of Outstanding Natural Beauty, Housman's "blue remembered hills" and the main focus for walkers in the county.

The AONB conveniently divides into several distinct chunks of hill country. From the Wrekin you can clearly see how four of them – Stiperstones, Long Mynd, Stretton Hills and Wenlock Edge – run roughly parallel in a south-west/north-east alignment. Independent of this pattern are the Clee Hills and the rolling uplands of Clun Forest.

Each of these blocks of high land has its own distinct character, as does each river valley which divides them, and that is one of the hallmarks of Shropshire, a county infinitely varied in its appeal. True, it lacks a coastline, and none of its hills quite attains the stature of a mountain, but it has just about every other desirable feature and surely is one of the most diverse, beautiful and deeply rural of all English counties. It's also one of the least known, but discerning souls who do come to know it almost invariably grow to love it too. It may lack the more dramatic landscapes found further north, but there is something about Shropshire which draws you back again and again.

The Tea Shops

Tea is seen as essentially English, but that's more to do with the fervour with which we adopted it than with its origins. The story begins nearly 5000 years ago in China when, in the year 2750BC, a twig from a tea bush accidentally fell into Emperor Shen Nung's bowl of boiled water. Well, it's a nice story, and true or not, tea is certainly Chinese in origin and didn't reach Europe until the seventeenth century. It was introduced by Portuguese traders and Charles II acquired a taste for it while exiled in the Netherlands. He was responsible for introducing it to Britain on his restoration to the throne in 1661, and so keen on it was he (or so valuable was it) that he accepted several cases of tea as part of the dowry when he married Catherine de Braganza, a Portuguese princess. Tea remained expensive, increasingly so after heavy taxation was introduced, leading to smuggling and black market trading, and it was many years before poorer people were able to afford it.

Today, however, it is drunk by almost everyone in the British Isles, and with enormous enthusiasm by many. Despite the increased popularity of coffee, tea is still seen as our national drink, and tea shops abound throughout the country. Pubs are still far commoner in rural areas but, even so, there is an increasing probability that you will be able to find a tea shop of one kind or another when enjoying a country walk, and there is nothing pleasanter than combining the two.

All the tea shops in this book fulfil certain criteria and all have been visited by the author. A letter and questionnaire were sent to all proprietors whose establishments seemed worth inclusion and the response to this was the final basis on which a choice was made. You can be certain, therefore (barring a change of ownership), that walkers are welcome at all these tea shops. However, please be considerate if wearing muddy boots and dripping waterproofs. Children are also welcome at all of them, though one proprietor did specify well-behaved children only. Dogs are not generally welcome (because of hygiene regulations) but there are a few exceptions to this rule, and where this is the case it is specified.

Smoking is permitted at very few but these are not specified as policy on smoking does change. Telephone numbers are given, however, for those who wish to check such details. It can also be advisable to check opening hours as these are often flexible.

One item in the questionnaire concerned provision for vegetarians and most proprietors responded positively to this, indicating that they do cater for vegetarians. However, when further
details were supplied it became clear that the concept is not
always fully understood – some proprietors, for instance, believe
that a certain margarine, which can contain gelatine, is more
acceptable to vegetarians than butter. Nothing could be further
from the truth. There is also much confusion concerning vegetarian cheeses, which are simply those made without animal rennet,
and are now widely available.

In a few of the tea shops in this book it is possible for vegetarians to be absolutely confident that they will be eating only what
is acceptable to them – consult the individual entries to discover
which. At others it would be advisable for strict vegetarians to
ask for details. In all of them, however, there is likely to be
something which is acceptable, even if the choice is more restricted than for non-vegetarians.

The Walks

A glance at the map showing the distribution of the walks will
instantly reveal an imbalance between north and south. This is
not just because the south of the county is more popular with
walkers, but is also due to various other factors, such as the
density of the footpath network. There are, for instance, very few
public footpaths in the north-east corner of the county, which
has always comprised large agricultural estates, and there are also
fewer areas with open access in the north. Tea shops are thin on
the ground too, and even where tea shops were found in the
northern half of the county there was a surprising lack of response
from many proprietors. The situation is very different south of
Shrewsbury and Telford, and the final choice of walks reflects
this.

There is no shortage of variety with these walks, which will
introduce you to many of Shropshire's different aspects. None of
the walks is particularly demanding for most averagely fit people,

and many are very gentle indeed. It's still as well to be properly equipped, although there's no need to invest your life savings in state-of-the-art gear. Common sense is the best guide, which means taking waterproofs with you, and sufficient layers of warm clothing in winter. It's best not to wear jeans if rain threatens as they're uncomfortable when wet and slow to dry. Proper walking boots are by no means necessary for all the walks in this book, but they do provide good ankle support, and they keep your feet dry in wet or muddy conditions (almost all the walks are potentially very muddy in winter).

A small rucksack is the best way of carrying spare gear, but it doesn't have to be an expensive, highly specified affair – you can get an adequate one for a few pounds. Carry food and drink if venturing into the hills on one of the longer, more demanding walks.

OS maps are invaluable. The directions in this book should ensure you don't get lost, but maps enable you to make changes to the given route, to identify distant hills and to put the local scene in context. Landrangers are fine for an overview, but the more detailed Pathfinders and Explorers are superb companions on any walk. They help you to identify puzzling landscape features, such as prehistoric cultivation terraces or deserted Medieval villages, and they make route-finding easy, even showing which side of a hedge a footpath runs. The Pathfinder series is currently being replaced by the new Explorers, but none is yet available for Shropshire.

The directions given should enable you to complete the walks without any difficulty, but bear in mind that things do change in the countryside – trees get blown over, hedges get ripped out, stiles get moved and cottages get knocked down. Any of these can make the directions invalid, but most paths are now waymarked (yellow arrows for footpaths, blue ones for bridleways) and are fairly easy to follow. Please note that where the directions indicate something along the lines of "climb a stile and go diagonally right" this assumes that, having climbed the stile, you are standing with your back to it.

Any obstuctions or other footpath problems should be reported to: The Rights of Way Officer, Countryside Service, Shropshire County Council, Column House, 7 London Road, Shrewsbury SY2 6NW.

The Shropshire Way

On several of the walks you'll find you are following a section of the Shropshire Way. This is a long distance path of 172 miles which was pioneered by Shropshire groups of the Ramblers' Association. It links most of the county's finest countryside and is a circular walk with a linear extension northwards from Wem to the Cheshire border at Grindley Brook. The Shropshire Way is waymarked with a buzzard logo and the buzzard's head indicates the direction of travel, in the same way as an arrow does. The choice of a buzzard is particularly appropriate as a symbol for Shropshire, as this magnificent bird of prey is becoming increasingly common in the county. You are certain to see many of them if you complete the walks in this book, though they are currently most numerous in the area around Craven Arms.

The Jack Mytton Way

This medium distance path is encountered on a few of the walks. It's a 70-mile bridleway between Rays Farm (featured in the Billingsley walk) and Llanfair Waterdine on the Powys border. Jack Mytton lived from 1796 to 1834 and was a colourful character, though hardly an admirable one, who became MP for Shrewsbury. He was a drunk and a gambler, given to wild exploits and crazy practical jokes, who wasted a large fortune and died of a stroke, aged 38, in a debtors' prison in London.

The Severn Way

This one is incomplete, but the ultimate aim is a path which follows the Severn from source to sea. Much of Shropshire's share of the Severn Way is easily walkable and you will encounter it on several of the walks in this book, especially in the Bridgnorth area. Around Ironbridge it seems to be known as the Severn Valley Way.

Shropshire Wildlife Trust

The Trust owns nature reserves throughout the county and has a policy of open access to most of them. The Trust's aims are to protect and enhance Shropshire's wildlife and habitats and to ensure public recognition of the need for a healthy environment managed on sustainable principles. To join the Trust, or for further details, contact: Shropshire Wildlife Trust, 167 Frankwell, Shrewsbury SY3 8LG. (Telephone 01743 241691)

Public Transport

Surely all country walkers must have noticed that it's now almost impossible, in England and Wales, to escape the sound of traffic? Or to find a view unspoilt by cars? Or a village not choked by them? And who has not gone back to somewhere they once loved, only to find it no longer exists, but has been replaced by a huge swathe of tarmac by-passing some traffic-battered little country town? With the Countryside Commission predicting a doubling, or even trebling, of rural traffic, things can only get worse. People talk of spending time in the countryside to find "peace and quiet" and to "get away from it all" and yet they go there by car, thereby helping to destroy the very thing they're in search of, and providing ammunition for the arguments of those who would build yet more by-passes.

It's still perfectly possible to get around on public transport. I've been exploring Shropshire by bus for the last 12 years, and all the walks in this book were accessed by public transport. Services are sometimes poor, but we get the public transport we deserve. If we use it, the demand will encourage the provision of extra services. If we don't use it, we'll lose it altogether.

Information about services is easily obtained. Shropshire County Council has a telephone enquiry line and publishes free timetable books which cover the county area by area. You can pick these up at tourist information centres, libraries and bus station travel centres (Shrewsbury, Oswestry and Telford). The aim is to revise them twice a year, but monthly updates detailing any changes are also published – look for these in tourist information centres, libraries, travel centres, Citizens' Advice Bureaux and District Council offices. Changes are also announced on local radio. Individual travel operators also have enquiry lines and publish their own timetables. In addition, many libraries, tourist information centres, travel centres and rail stations have copies of the Great Britain Bus Timetable (published by Southern Vectis Bus Company, Newport, Isle of Wight) and the National Express timetable.

Information about bus and train services is given for each walk, but as it would be impractical to list all bus services only the main ones are specified. If you consult timetables you will often find additional services. Remember that you don't necessarily need a bus to the given starting point of a walk; any point along the route will do – and is, indeed, often preferable to a starting point dictated by the need to park a car.

The Severn Valley Railway

It's worth noting that rail travellers in Shropshire are not restricted to mainline services only. The Severn Valley Railway provides professionally run steam services between Bridgnorth and Kidderminster, connecting with mainline services at the latter. Trains run several times daily from May to October and there are reduced services for the rest of the year. Both trains and stations are beautifully kept, with refreshments usually available, and the line runs through delightful countryside.

Useful phone numbers

Shropshire Traveline (8am-6pm Mon-Sat) 0345 056785
Train, Bus and Coach Hotline (6am-9pm daily) 0891 910910
National Rail Enquiries (24 hours daily) 0345 484950
National Express (8am-10pm daily) 0990 808080

Walk 1: Shrewsbury

Start: Montford Bridge. Grid reference 433153. This is a linear walk ending in Shrewsbury. Montford Bridge is served by Midland Red D70 which runs between Shrewsbury and Oswestry Monday to Saturday. An adult single fare from Shrewsbury to Montford Bridge is currently 75 pence.

Summary: An easy and very pleasant walk on the Severn Way, though not all of it is beside the river. There are no hills but you may have to clamber over about a dozen stiles and padlocked gates. The walk takes you into Shrewsbury through some of the most attractive parts of town.

Length: 6 miles.

Maps: OS Landranger 126, OS Pathfinder 869.

Parking: Public car parks in Shrewsbury, e.g. Raven Meadows.

Trains: Daily services on Birmingham-Aberystwyth/Chester line, Cardiff- Manchester/Liverpool line and Swansea-Shrewsbury (Heart of Wales) line.

Buses: Numerous services to Shrewsbury from the rest of Shropshire and surrounding counties. Daily National Express coaches from Aberystwyth, Birmingham, London, Wrexham etc. Service to Montford Bridge as above.

The Tea Shop

The Oscars Café and Bistro, The Music Hall, The Square, Shrewsbury.

It would be hard to find a town of comparable size with a better range of tempting places to eat and drink than Shrewsbury. The Oscars scores highly in several respects, however. For a start, it's conveniently situated next to the tourist information centre in the Music Hall, an imposing building in The Square. You can sit and look out through elegantly draped sash windows at the old market hall and other notable buildings, as well as at the constant comings and goings of residents, visitors and tourists, many of whom find The Square an ideal place to relax for a while. There are separate menus for lunch and morning coffee/afternoon tea. The lunch menu includes a range of grills, roasts and snacks, but what sets it apart is the superb serve-yourself salad bar. Salads are included in the price of most dishes and you can pile your plate high. Dishes suitable for vegetarians are marked as such on the menu – vegetarian cheese is used and vegetable stock for soup. The morning coffee/afternoon tea menu includes a range of traditional cakes, scones, sandwiches and pastries as well as ice cream.

Open: 10am-5pm Monday-Saturday all year, also 10am-4pm Sundays from Spring Bank Holiday until end of September. Telephone: 01743 358057.

The Walk

Shrewsbury is not the largest town in Shropshire, but it is the county town and has always been the focal point for trade and commerce. In 1300 a census showed it to be one of the twelve most prosperous towns in England. That's no longer the case, but it is certainly one of the most attractive, with an astonishing wealth of period buildings. Most of these are crowded together in the town centre, on what is almost an island formed by a loop of the Severn. Away from the centre, Shrewsbury is, like most towns, less appealing, girdled as it is by ring roads and almost suffocated by suburbs, but there is a gap in all this on the north-west side of town, and it's this gap which provides the key to this very pleasant walk.

Catch the D70 from the bus station (or from Oswestry) and alight on the Shrewsbury side of Montford Bridge. The bridge, designed by Thomas Telford in 1792, spans the Severn and this is an ancient river crossing which was often the scene of bloodshed in the days when cross-border raids were a regular feature of Shropshire life.

Walk towards the bridge and, a few dozen metres from the bus stop, you'll see the Severn Way signposted on the right, opposite

English Bridge spanning the River Severn, Shrewsbury

the Wingfield Arms. Go more or less straight ahead by the right-hand edge of a cow pasture, with the River Severn on your left. Continue across an arable field then over a stile into sheep pasture. Walk up a slight rise, then pass to the right of a hedgerow to reach a stile and gate.

Join a tree-lined green lane which eventually passes an overgrown, seemingly abandoned graveyard to join a lane at Bicton. Go straight on past Bicton Hall and continue until the lane bends right. Leave it here, going through a gate to rejoin the bridleway. Keep straight on and as you approach Grove Farm you'll see two gates into the yard. Go through the left-hand one and straight on, joining a lane.

When you reach a junction, climb two stiles by the side of Rossall Lodge then bear left to a pond. Stand with your back to it and bear left across a meadow towards a clump of trees. As you draw nearer you'll see two stiles. Go over the first (right-hand) one and proceed by the hedgerow to a waymarked post then bear slightly right across an arable field and through a gap in the far hedge. Keep straight on to pass to the right of woodland then continue by the hedge. Ignore a footpath which branches left and keep going past Spring Coppice until a stile gives access to a track. Follow the track to a road at Shelton. Turn left on a footway for a few yards then back onto the bridleway which takes a lovely route through a tree-lined holloway before returning you to the road. Turn left on a narrow path beside sheep pasture on top of the cliffs which fall away to the Severn. The path quite soon descends steps to the riverbank and follows the river closely for nearly a mile.

When the path ends, climb a flight of steps and turn left, walking between attractive houses and their cliff-top gardens, detached from them by the footpath. Before long, steps descend once more to the river and the footpath soon emerges into open grassland at Mountfields. Look out for a waymarked post which sends you to the right towards a stile near a group of willows. Walk through a strip of woodland to open grassland and keep left, following a willow-lined brook back to the Severn. Go to the right, passing tall poplar trees and, in the spring, masses of daffodils. A footbridge soon looms ahead and, beyond it, a road bridge, but it's best to stay on the west bank until you come to a third bridge, Port Hill footbridge, just after the Boathouse Inn. Erected in 1922, it's a green-painted suspension bridge which takes you across the Severn to The Quarry, a popular riverside park. The direct route from here to The Square is straight ahead through the park and along Claremont Hill, right at the crossroads on Bellstone, left at the next junction on Shoplatch then right on Market Street to The Square. Alternatively, just follow signs for the tourist information centre. However, a thorough exploration of Shrewsbury is recommended, as is the purchase of a town trail booklet from the tourist information centre.

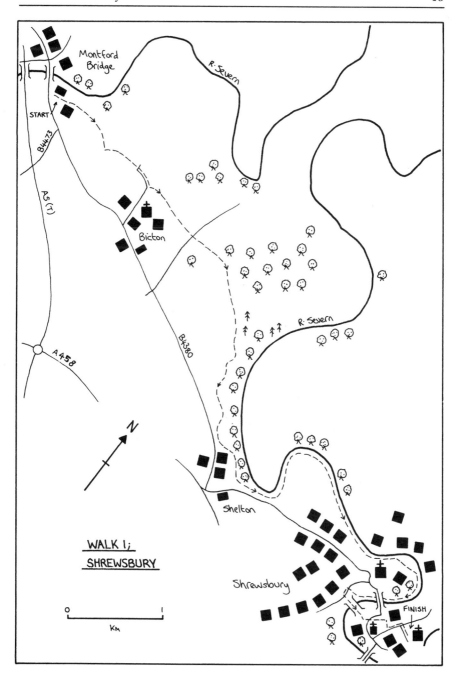

Walk 2: Oswestry

Start: Oswestry Heritage Centre. Grid reference 288293.

Summary: Mixed terrain, with mostly woodland and pasture. Though a longer walk, it's undemanding, with only a few gentle slopes and not too many stiles. It includes two impressive ancient monuments, Offa's Dyke and Hên Dinas.

Length: 10 miles.

Maps: OS Landranger 126, OS Pathfinders 827 and 847.

Parking: Public car parks in Oswestry, e.g. Beatrice Street.

Trains: Daily trains on Birmingham-Aberystwyth/Chester line to Gobowen (2½ miles from Oswestry) with bus link (there is some hope that Oswestry station may soon reopen).

Buses: Midland Red D70 from Shrewsbury; Monday-Saturday. Williamsons 576 from Shrewsbury; Monday-Saturday. Midland Red D53/63 from Ellesmere/Gobowen; Monday-Saturday. Midland Red D71 from Welshpool; Monday-Saturday. Midland Red 2/2A from Wrexham/Gobowen; daily. Tanat Valley 449 from Ellesmere; Monday-Saturday. National Express coaches from Birmingham, London, Wrexham etc; daily.

The Tea Shop

Oswestry Heritage and Exhibition Centre, 2 Church Terrace, Oswestry.

The tea shop is owned by the town council and housed in a timber-framed building which serves mainly as a heritage and exhibition centre. It was formerly a grammar school, founded by David Holbache in 1407, which makes it the second oldest in the country (Winchester was founded 20 years earlier). It's an attractive building pleasantly situated in St Oswald's churchyard. Inside, oak beams and panelling create just the right atmosphere to enjoy the home-cooked local food on offer, including Oswestry specialities such as hand-raised pie. Or choose from scones, cakes, sandwiches, pizza, quiche, pasta or jacket potatoes. Appropriately, for this border town, delicious Welsh cakes are available too. Vegetarian meals are included on the menu, and soups are made with vegetable stock. Free range eggs are used and cakes are made with sunflower margarine. Pastries, however, may contain lard. Though dogs are not allowed in the tea room, the centre's supervisor, Sue Ellis, says they can be tied up outside or taken to a patio area in summer and they will always be offered a drink of water. Sue recommends a couple of short walks from the centre – the town trail or a visit to Plas Wilmot, the house where war poet Wilfred Owen was born.

Open: 9.30am-4.30pm Monday-Saturday in summer; 10am-3.30pm Monday-Saturday in winter (also closed Thursdays January-Easter). Telephone: 01691 671323.

The Walk

To see Oswestry at its lively best try visiting on a Wednesday or a summer Saturday when the market is held. On any day of the week, however, it's a friendly, bustling small town with many interesting buildings. There are also the scant remains of a motte and bailey castle in the town centre – now just a large mound and a few bits of masonry in a public park behind Bailey Head. The origins of the castle are unknown but it was rebuilt in 1148 by Madoc ap Meredydd and saw plenty of action before peace finally descended on the Marches. It was refortified in the Civil War when Oswestry was a Royalist stronghold. The Roundheads successfully besieged the castle and then destroyed it.

The Heritage Centre is at the southern end of town off Church Street. Neighbouring St Oswald's Church is basically thirteenth century, but was partly rebuilt in the 1690s and again in the 1870s. After visiting the church and Heritage Centre walk to the nearby crossroads and turn right along Upper Brook Street, then right again into Oswald's Place. You'll soon pass Oswald's Well, an important site in the town's history. Oswald was King of Northumbria in 641, when he was defeated in battle by Penda, King of Mercia, at what is now Oswestry. Oswald was killed and his body nailed to a tree but an eagle carried off one of his arms only to drop it. Where it fell a spring burst forth from the earth and the water proved to have healing properties. Or so the story goes. . . The name Oswestry is derived from "Oswald's Tree".

When you come to a waterworks turn left, then right at a T-junction. After 100 metres cross to a well-defined footpath running across park-like pastureland. After crossing a lane the path continues as a farm track.

Pass through a wood then keep left of ruined Llanforda Hall. Re-enter pastureland and, once over the next stile, fork right, but stay in the pasture; don't be tempted by a gate on the side of a slope.

Pass through a gate labelled "Llanforda Estate Footpath" and after a short distance fork right. The path curves round into a plantation and you should keep to this main path, ignoring any turnings, as it eventually passes between boulders into a dense stand of conifers.

Very soon you emerge into beautiful open woodland as your path is joined by Offa's Dyke National Trail. This runs for 170 miles from Prestatyn to Chepstow, partly following the earthwork constructed by Offa, King of Mercia, in the eighth century – either as a fortification or simply a demarcation of the border.

Continue through the woods to a bracken-covered common with splendid views of the Welsh mountains. From 1777 to 1848 this was a race course; it's now a popular site for walks and picnics. Keep straight on and you'll soon go over a staggered crossroads. With Offa's Dyke Path now on your left, follow the obvious course of the former race track which soon curves to the right between a pond and Chapel House. Leave the race track for a well-trodden path on the left. Take the third of three signposted footpaths, just beyond a house. Go through a plantation then cross a field, with good views of Hên Dinas (the hillfort) below.

Join a track, turning right, then right again at a T-junction. After half a mile join a footpath on the left which passes Brogyntyn Farm, goes through a wood then continues as a tree-lined avenue through pastureland, part of Brogyntyn Park, the property of Lord Harlech. After passing Brogyntyn Hall, an imposing mansion dating from around 1730, continue over more pasture to the road.

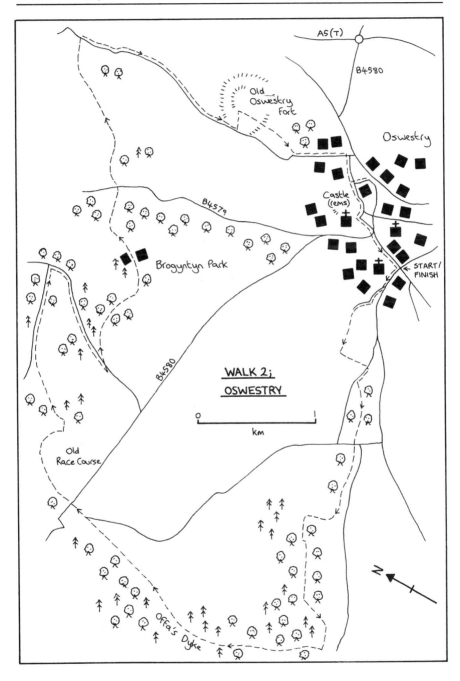

A5(T)

B4580

Old
Oswestry
Fort

Oswestry

B4579

Castle
(rems)

START/
FINISH

Brogyntyn Park

B4580

WALK 2;
OSWESTRY

0   1
km

Old
Race Course

Offa's Dyke

N

Cross to another footpath opposite and keep straight on for three-quarters of a mile, ignoring all turnings. Turn right when you come to a lane. Very soon Hên Dinas, also known as Old Oswestry, comes into view, and some distance along the lane a gate gives access to the fort. With its huge, well-defined ramparts and ditches it's one of the most outstanding Iron Age forts in the country. It was first occupied about 300BC, by the Cornovii people, but went through at least four phases of development. It was abandoned after the Roman Conquest but probably reoccupied when the legions withdrew. Visible from its ramparts is the line of Wat's Dyke, an earthen fortification which probably predated Offa's Dyke and can be traced sporadically from Oswestry to the Dee Estuary.

Having explored the fort, walk through the adjacent Llwyn Coppice to rejoin the lane and continue into Oswestry, emerging almost opposite the bus station and car park at the end of Beatrice Street.

The massive earthworks at Hen Dinas, Oswestry, Shropshire

Walk 3: Ellesmere

Start: Mereside, Ellesmere. Grid reference 407345.

Summary: There's a very watery theme to this walk, which includes not only three meres but also a stretch of the Llangollen Canal. As you would expect, it's mainly level going but there are a few gentle undulations near the start. The paths are clear and easy to follow, with about a dozen stiles, and the scenery is lovely.

Length: 7 miles.

Maps: OS Landranger 126, OS Pathfinder 828.

Parking: The Moors car park at Mereside or in town centre, e.g. Talbot Street. Or at The Boathouse – but please ask permission first.

Trains: Nearest station is Gobowen (7 miles).

Buses: Midland Red D53 from Oswestry via Gobowen; Monday-Saturday. Tanat Valley 449 from Oswestry; Monday-Saturday. Midland Red 501 from Shrewsbury; Tuesday, Wednesday, Friday.

The Tea Shop

The Boathouse, Mereside, Ellesmere.

The Boathouse is situated on the edge of The Mere so you can sit outside in the garden and watch the swans and ducks on the water while you enjoy a snack from the tempting range on offer. Alternatively, sit indoors and relax in the unusual ambience of this 1930s building, recently restored to a high standard, with polished wood floors, oak beams and three woodburning stoves. Choose from soups, sandwiches, baked potatoes, toasted sandwiches, cakes, pastries or scones. There are also daily specials and a good choice of drinks. Vegetarians are catered for to some extent, in that soup is made with vegetable stock and cakes etc are made with vegetable margarine. However, neither vegetarian cheese nor free range eggs are used.

Dogs are welcome in the garden only.

Open: 10am-6pm daily April-September, but closed Monday and
Tuesday October-March. Telephone: 01691 623828.

The Walk

Ellesmere is an attractive little market town which is not always
explored by the many visitors who flock to The Mere. Yet it has
some lovely period buildings, not only in the centre but also in
the quieter back streets, with their wealth of Georgian and Victorian houses.

If you do explore the town you can reach The Mere via Water-
gate Street or, better still, St John's Hill, which takes you past the
parish church – you can get down to The Mere here or continue
along Sandy Lane until a stile gives access to Castlefields and a
footpath to The Mere. Castlefields is the site of a motte and bailey
castle built by Roger de Montgomery in the late eleventh century.
Nothing remains of the castle itself but the earthworks are still
clearly visible. There is a superb view of The Mere from this

Cottage at Ellesmere

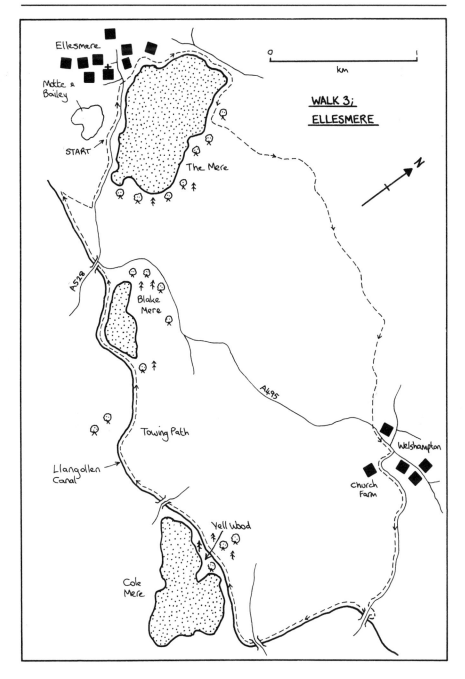

vantage point and the field is managed as a haymeadow to encourage wild flowers and butterflies. A little further along Sandy Lane is Plantation Wood, managed by Shropshire Wildlife Trust and open to the public.

The Mere is the best known of Shropshire's meres but despite all the human visitors, it still attracts large numbers of water birds, and is especially important for winter migrants such as wigeon, pochard, goosander and teal. It also has a large heronry occupied by breeding birds in spring and early summer. The surrounding woodlands are important for birds too, and the whole area is managed for its wildlife value as well as for public recreation. Mereside itself is immensely popular but it's worth staying a while, not only to sample the delights of the Boathouse, but also to call in at the visitor centre. You can find out about Shropshire's meres and mosses here, as well as the usual range of tourist information, and there are books and maps on sale.

To begin the walk head north beside The Mere (ie if you're standing facing it you need to go to the left) and into Cremorne Gardens. A very pleasant path runs through trees close by the water's edge for about three-quarters of a mile and then enters a meadow. There is a lovely view from here across The Mere to St Mary's Church at Ellesmere. Turn left here, and follow the yellow arrows along the edges of two fields. Bear left in the third field, aiming for a signpost near a farm, where a stile leads to a track and you go straight on, soon entering a field. Leave the track and walk straight up a bank to a stile. Go straight on over an arable field to another stile then turn right on a track.

The route is clearly defined as you cross a succession of fields and it's impossible to go wrong. Before long you'll find yourself in a field which narrows to a point. After leaving this keep straight on by the hedge in the next field and when the hedge turns a corner go with it, soon joining a green lane and then another track. Keep on in the same direction to reach a road on the edge of Welshampton. Turn left and go straight on at a junction, passing a school and a church then turning right on Lyneal Lane.

When you come, after about three-quarters of a mile, to a bridge over the Llangollen Canal, descend steps to the towpath and turn right, passing under the bridge. The Llangollen is a branch of the Shropshire Union Canal, fondly known as the Shroppie, which was planned to link Chester, the River Mersey and the River Severn. The Llangollen branch was constructed by the Ellesmere Canal Company between 1793 and 1805, supervised by Thomas Telford from offices in Beech House in Ellesmere, now the main British Waterways yard. Ellesmere gave its name to the town which grew up around the Shroppie's Mersey terminus – Ellesmere Port.

Soon after passing under bridge 53 at Lyneal Wharf you'll see woodland on the other side of the canal, and glimpses of an expanse of water through the trees. This is Colemere, which is a Site of Special Scientific Interest but also a country park, therefore another place, like The Mere, where wildlife has to coexist with leisure use. Colemere supports a wide range of aquatic life, and Yell Wood, which borders the canal, consists mainly of native broad-leaved trees, although there are also some alien conifers and rhododendron, which are gradually being removed. There is a footpath round Colemere but there is no official access from the towpath, although local walkers make their way to it via bridge 54 (Yell Bridge).

Continuing along the towpath, you'll soon pass lovely Blakemere, separated from the towpath only by a narrow strip of woodland and immensely scenic in the beautiful light of early morning.

After leaving Blakemere behind you pass through the Ellesmere Tunnel, which is 80 metres long. Take care as the ground is uneven in places. Once through the tunnel press on along the towpath until a signpost indicates The Moors car park at Mereside to your right and the town centre straight ahead along the towpath. The choice is yours, but it is rewarding to follow the town arm to the wharf at its terminus.

Walk 4: Whitchurch

Start: High Street, Whitchurch. Grid reference 542416.

Summary: An undemanding walk in gently undulating dairy country. A short stretch of the Llangollen Canal is explored and Whitchurch itself is worth an hour or more, as there are some interesting buildings lining its streets. The paths are mostly easy to follow but you do have to cross the by-pass (A41). There are about a dozen stiles.

Length: 5 miles.

Maps: OS Landranger 117, OS Pathfinder 807.

Parking: Public car parks in Whitchurch, e.g. behind High Street.

Trains: Daily services on the Cardiff-Manchester/Liverpool line.

Buses: Midland Red 221/222 from Wem; Monday-Saturday. North West Road Car Company from Chester; Monday-Saturday.

The Tea Shop

Walker's, 21/23 High Street, Whitchurch.

Walker's is one of the most attractive and distinctive buildings on the High Street, with timber-framing above a traditional shop front. The ground floor is a traditional baker's shop and the tea shop is upstairs. Oak-beamed, warm and welcoming, it provides a good range of snacks which come in generous portions. All-day breakfasts are available, along with baked potatoes, soups, cakes, pastries, toasted sandwiches, cream teas and much more. Vegetarians are catered for.

Open: 9am-4.30pm Monday to Saturday. Telephone: 01948 664687.

The Walk

Whitchurch is an appealing market town with many fine Medieval, Tudor, Georgian and Victorian buildings. It's one of the oldest continually inhabited towns in the country and was occupied by

Walker's of Whitchurch

the Romans who named it Mediolanum and valued it for its strategic location at the heart of their road network. It later became renowned for its clocks, made by the firm of J B Joyce, established in 1690. They make magnificent clocks which have gained an international reputation and can be found on cathedrals and palaces worldwide. There are examples of Joyce's work in the town. Whitchurch is also a centre of the dairy industry and cheese fairs were a regular feature in the past.

The Llangollen Canal passes within a mile of the town centre and the Whitchurch Arm is in the process of being restored and reopened, forming part of a major project that will include the creation of the only working inclined plane in the country, along with a leisure lake and country park.

Begin your walk by making your way up to the top end of High Street (towards the church) and turning left on Yardington, a street occupying the line of a town wall built at the end of the second century when the Romans were in control of Whitchurch.

It was excavated during road widening in 1977 and beneath it were found the earlier defences of a series of Roman forts built on the site in the first century.

On reaching a roundabout turn right on Sherrymill Hill and continue for about 200 metres until you see a footpath on the right, by a post box. Follow the path to a junction where you turn left. Cross an area of rough ground, with a brook on your left, and keep going on a well-used path which skirts a new housing estate to meet a road. Turn right until the road bends right then join a footpath over grassland on the left. The path curves right to a stile and then climbs slightly, running along a slight ridge above the valley.

When you eventually come to a stile and footbridge turn right, soon crossing to the other side of a fence by a large beech tree and bearing right to another stile. Bear left to another then turn right to the next. Descend to the by-pass and cross with care, joining a footpath almost opposite.

Climb a stile and walk towards a derelict barn then turn left to Danson's Bridge, spanning the Llangollen Canal. Cross and turn right, going over two stiles to join the towpath then turning left beside the canal. The Llangollen is a branch of the Shropshire Union and though it was scheduled for closure in the 1940s, it's now one of the most popular canals with leisure boaters.

Before long you'll reach Grindley Brook, with its locks and wharf. If you need a break there is a pub, the Horse and Jockey, on the main road, though Grindley Brook, blighted as it is by the A41, is probably not a place which will tempt you to linger. Yet this rather unprepossessing spot is important to walkers. Just metres from the border with Cheshire, it is the starting point for the Shropshire Way and the Sandstone Trail. The latter runs for just over 30 miles to Beacon Hill above Frodsham, following the Central Cheshire Ridge, with fine views all the way. Both the Maelor Way and the South Cheshire Way also pass through Grindley Brook.

In fact, it is this latter which is your route now; cross the canal

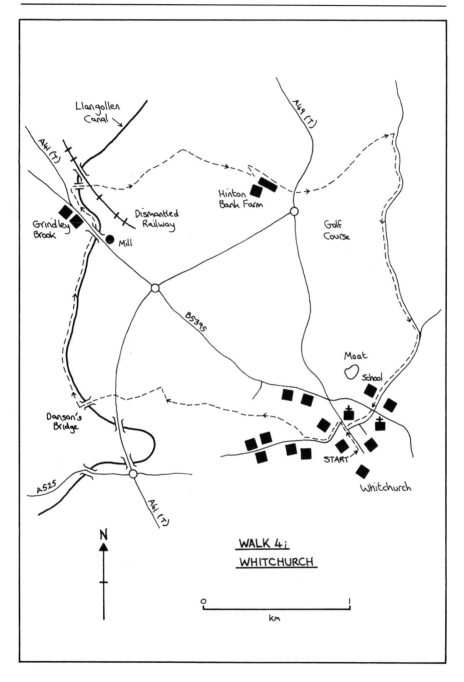

WALK 4;
WHITCHURCH

by bridge 28 at Lane Croft Wharf and continue on a bridleway, passing under a railway then going through a gate at a signpost for the South Cheshire Way. Cross a field to another gate just to the left of a farm and then keep straight on by field edges. The bridleway soon becomes a well-defined green lane, sunken by long use below the level of the surrounding fields.

As you approach Hinton Bank Farm, go through a waymarked gate on the left and walk up to a track. Turn right and pass to the left of Hinton Bank to reach a road. The bridleway continues opposite along an access drive. As you reach the entrance to a house fork left, still on the bridleway, and keep going to reach Terrick Road. Turn right along this lovely lane, passing Terrick Farm and Terrick Hall Hotel. After passing a golf club the lane is less pleasant, due to increased traffic, but you soon reach a junction where you turn right for the final stretch into Whitchurch. At a junction with the main road go straight ahead on Claypit Street to St Alkmund's church. Built of red sandstone in 1712-13 by William Smith, after the collapse of its Medieval predecessor, this is the largest eighteenth-century church in the county, outside Shrewsbury. The west tower has a balustrade and pinnacles and a semi-circular porch attached to it, and there are some interesting memorials inside.

Walk 5: Wem

Start: Wem station. Grid reference 517290. This is a linear walk between rail stations. Travel by train, bus or car to Wem, walk to Yorton and get the train back to Wem, or to your home station. Note that Yorton station is a request stop, so you must signal the driver, just as you would when catching a bus. Likewise, if intending to alight at Yorton you must inform the conductor.

Summary: The highlight of the walk is Grinshill, a sandstone outcrop popular with local people. The descent from Grinshill is steep but otherwise this is a walk of very gentle gradients. It's mainly on the Shropshire Way and the paths are easy to follow, except on Grinshill itself. There are 15 stiles.

Length: 6 miles.

Maps: OS Landranger 126, OS Pathfinder 848.

Parking: Yorton station; also public car parks in Wem, e.g. Leek Street.

Trains: Daily services on Cardiff-Manchester/Liverpool line.

Buses: Midland Red 221/222 from Whitchurch; Monday-Saturday. Midland Red/Boultons 511 from Shrewsbury; Monday-Saturday

The Tea Shop

Tudor Coffee Shop, Leek Street, Wem.

Not, despite its name, a riot of timber-framing and old oak settles. But it is warm and cosy, with friendly service and low prices. It's popular with locals and conveniently situated where High Street meets Aston Street (which leads to the station). A good choice of lunches and snacks is on offer, including some tempting cakes, scones and pastries. The latter are made with vegetable margarine and vegetable stock is used for soups.

Open: 9am-4.30pm Monday-Saturday. Telephone: 01939 290978.

The Walk

Wem is a traditional market town with many interesting, if unspectacular, buildings to admire. Few of them are very old because the town was almost demolished in 1643 during the Civil War when a band of 40 Parliamentarians defeated an attacking force of 5,000 Royalists. Much more destruction followed in 1677 when an unfortunate 14-year old, Jane Churm, accidentally set alight the thatch roof of her home. The resulting "Great Fire of Wem" destroyed over 140 buildings in just an hour. A few Medieval buildings did survive, and some of the best, such as Astley House, are found in Noble Street.

A town trail leaflet will help you explore Wem but for this walk go along the main street as far as the church then turn down Mill Street and proceed as far as the impressive buildings of Wem Mill. Turn right here on a well-defined footpath beside the River Roden. Follow the river for about half a mile until you come to an old bridge. Cross here and go through a small gate then straight ahead to the left of a tributary stream to reach a lane.

Turn left through the peaceful hamlet of Tilley, where there are some fine buildings, particularly timber-framed Tilley Manor and Tilley Hall. The latter, with two gabled wings guarding a recessed centre, bears the date 1613. On reaching a junction by another impressive house, Tilley Farm, keep straight on to cross the railway and then the main road. Proceed along the lane opposite, which leads to Tilley Green. Keep left at a junction then fork right at the next on a "no through road".

When you reach an attractive brick house named The Fields, climb a stile almost opposite to join the Shropshire Way. It's now just a question of following a succession of waymarked stiles over fields, a mixture of arable and pasture. The path is always clear, even if, in places, this appears to be achieved by the dubious practice of clearing a swathe with herbicide.

Before long you'll see the tall church spire at Clive, which you will be visiting later. But first the path keeps you to the left of it, heading towards the wooded eminence of Grinshill. On reaching

Tilley Manor

a track turn right, and shortly left into a field. Proceed to a green lane and go straight on across another field. On reaching a lane turn right to the edge of Clive then left over a stile. Follow the edge of a field to its corner and go through a gate or over a stile to the next field and left along its edge. Pass a cottage to reach a track and turn right, passing abandoned, overgrown quarries, then left into Corbet Wood.

You're now on the sandstone ridge of Grinshill, which has been quarried since Roman times. Until the mid-nineteenth century the stone was used only in Shropshire, but the construction of the railways meant it could be transported much further, so buildings of Grinshill stone came to grace many a town and city. It was used for several railway stations and for many of the grandiose building projects of Victorian Britain. Some quarrying still continues at Grinshill. Two types of sandstone are extracted – red and white. The latter is of much higher quality.

The hill is now also a popular place for recreation and a multitude of paths has developed so it can be very confusing. Just remember that basically you need to go down and then to the right and you're unlikely to go far wrong. The Shropshire Way is not much help as it's poorly waymarked, but it really doesn't matter if you wander off course as this is not a place where it's possible to be lost for very long.

Follow the main path into the woods and you should very soon see a small disused quarry on your right. A few yards after this there is a path leading steeply down on the left. This is one of the most direct ways down but first you may like to go to the top of Grinshill, which means continuing to the right on the main path and following it to the highest point. The shallow, sandy soil favours trees such as birch and rowan and there is a ground cover of bracken and bilberries, making this a delightful change from the intensively farmed landscape you've just crossed from Wem.

The very top of the hill is open grassland and there is a toposcope, erected on the occasion of the Queen's Silver Jubilee in 1977. Although you're only at 630ft (192m), the view includes the Wrekin, Wenlock Edge, the Clees, the Strettons, the Long Mynd, Jodrell Bank, the Peckforton Hills, the Arans, the Berwyns and Cader Idris (on a clear day!)

Retrace your steps to the descending path noted earlier and follow it down the slope. There are plenty of alternative paths so it's really a question of choosing the best way down and generally bearing to the right. At the bottom you should join a sunken, walled bridleway which goes to Grinshill village. Emerging by the village hall fork left on another track, Gooseberry Lane, which leads to the attractive main street. Turn right, and then very soon right again to the church. All Saints is a small Victorian building (1839-40) in neo-Norman style.

Continue up the track, going back towards the village hall but turning left before you reach it to walk below Grinshill Cliff on a sandy, walled bridleway. This lovely path leads to the church at Clive, which is best visited in early spring, when it rises above a sea of daffodils. However, it's impressive at any time because of the height of its spire, a landmark for many miles around. There

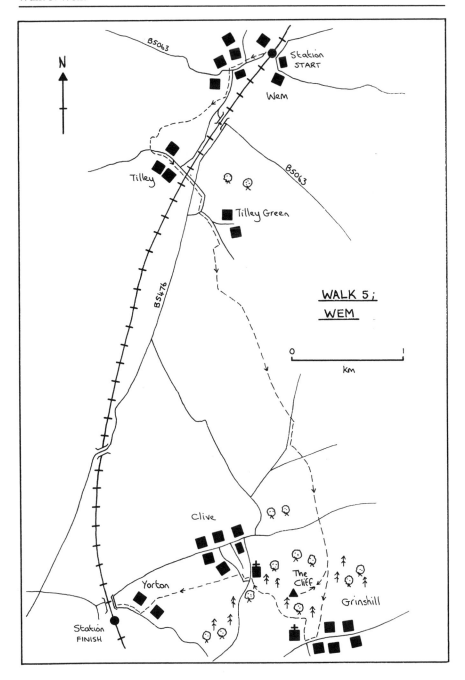

was a Norman church here originally but most of the present building is of 1885-94, though two Norman doorways survive. The Restoration dramatist, William Wycherley, born in 1640 at Clive Hall, is buried in the churchyard. The bridleway joins a lane just below the church. If you want to explore the village (and there are some lovely houses) turn right, but otherwise go straight on down Back Lane. Turn right by the village club then first left on a footpath. Beginning as a green lane, this leads to a sheep pasture where you keep straight on to go through a gate in the far right corner. A stile leads to the next field which you cross to reach a gate. Turn right along a lane to Yorton station.

Walk 6: Harmer Hill

Start: Pimhill Organic Farm Shop, Harmer Hill. Grid reference
           492212. Or Merrington Green, grid reference 465209. The
           directions below start from Pimhill.

Summary: An easy, delightful walk in mixed farming country. A high point
           of the walk is Merrington Green, a nature reserve with open
           access. The sandstone ridges at Pim Hill and Webscott are
           lovely too and provide variety in an otherwise largely flat land-
           scape. The quality of the footpaths is good and there are only
           eight stiles.

Length: 5 miles.

Maps: OS Landranger 126, OS Pathfinder 848.

Parking: Cars may be left at the farm shop. If you start at Merrington
           Green instead there is a car park at the grid reference above.

Trains: Nearest station is Yorton (1½ miles).

Buses: Williamsons 576 from Shrewsbury and Oswestry to Merrington
           Green; Monday-Saturday. Midland Red 501 from Shrewsbury
           and Ellesmere to Harmer Hill; Tuesday, Wednesday, Friday.

The Tea Shop

Pimhill Organic Farm Shop, Lea Hall, Harmer Hill.

In 1990 Richard Mayall became an MBE for services to agricul-
ture, yet in 1949, when he persuaded his father that they should
begin running the family farm organically, he was the subject of
local derision. His beliefs have long since been vindicated and
the farm, like many other organic farms, is flourishing. Richard
runs it in partnership with his daughter Ginny, who won the title
of Daily Express Young Countrywoman of the Year, also in 1990.
They have herds of Ayrshires and Holsteins, but the farm's main
produce is flour, milled from their own grain. This is sold in the
farm shop, along with a host of other products, most of them
bought in.

Pimhill Farm Shop (and Tea Shop)

The tea shop is tiny, with just a couple of tables on a gallery floor above the shop, and the choice is fairly basic – tea or coffee and a range of cakes and scones. But prices are low and everything is homemade and utterly delicious, and suitable for vegetarians too. In fact, this place is a delight. The range of organic foods on display is second to none, while outside there is much to admire, including two Tamworth pigs, Fred and Felix. Farm cats and peafowl wander about and if you visit the picnic area you'll see rabbits, pygmy goats, a donkey and some geese. It's all great fun for children but take care around the geese, which can be aggressive. Dogs are welcome, on a lead. Open: 10am-5pm Monday to Saturday. Telephone: 01939 290342.

The Walk

Begin by walking north on the wide verge beside the main road (A528). Fork right at a junction and proceed into Harmer Hill.

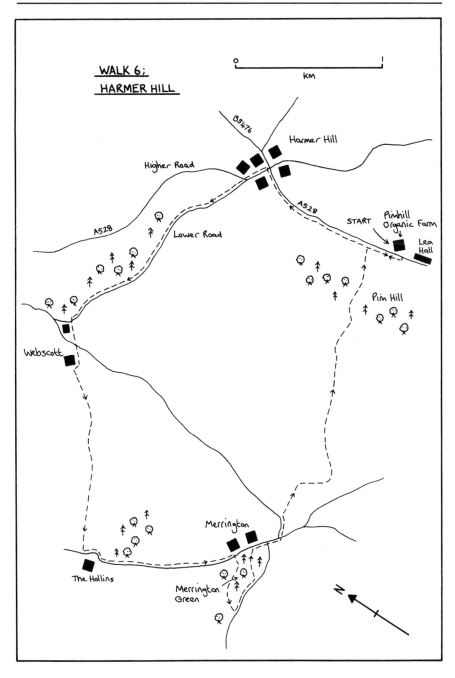

WALK 6;
HARMER HILL

KM

BS476

Harmer Hill

Higher Road

A528

START

Pinhill
Organic Farm

Lea
Hall

A528

Lower Road

Pim Hill

Webscott

Merrington

The Hollins

Merrington
Green

N

Look out for a cast iron milepost on the right, which directs you to Wem (4 miles) and Salop (6 miles). Though Salop is sometimes used as an alternative name for Shropshire, to local people it means Shrewsbury.

When you come to a crossroads turn left and go straight on at another crossroads, along Lower Road, leading to Webscott. Towering above the lane is a tree-covered and much-quarried sandstone ridge, across which there are many footpaths, both official and unofficial. It's well worth exploring but don't rely on OS maps (until updated) as some of the paths have been diverted; just follow the waymarkers instead.

There are a few houses along the lane and one of them, The Nest, is built into the cliff. A little further on you'll see stiles either side of the road. Cross the one on the left and walk straight ahead across fields to a lane, then along a bridleway opposite. After passing the barns of Webscott Farm the bridleway turns right towards the farmhouse then left to run through fields as a hard-surfaced track.

After half a mile you'll see a short length of unusually substantial hedgerow on your right. Once past it, go into a field and continue in the same direction, still in line with the farm track but about 50 metres to the right of it. Go through a bridle gate where a hedge and fence meet and proceed ahead to join a lovely, tree-lined green lane, bordered by masses of primroses in the spring. Turn left and walk to Merrington Green, where you'll see a green waymarker indicating a right turn.

This is not a right of way, but walkers are welcome to explore Merrington Green, a Shropshire Wildlife Trust reserve managed in partnership with Shrewsbury and Atcham Borough Council. Several paths have been waymarked, though there are also other paths branching off them. To explore the Green, follow this one, which passes between two pools, to a junction where you fork right. Do the same again at the next major junction and you will arrive at a small car park, where a map of the Green is displayed. This is a good alternative starting point for the walk, especially for anybody arriving by Williamson's bus, which stops here.

Merrington Green is a Medieval common with a good mix of habitats – woodland, scrub, grassland and ponds – and is frequented by a wide range of wildlife, particularly birds. Residents are augmented by species such as redwing and fieldfare in winter, while the summer months see an influx of visitors such as willow warbler, chiffchaff, blackcap and cuckoo. The Green is rich in pondlife too, with all three species of newt present, and good numbers of dragonflies and damselflies throughout the summer.

Walk through the car park towards the lane but turn left by a waymarked post. Go right at three junctions then turn left close beside the lane. There are surprisingly good views southwards over the countryside from this point. After passing a bench the path descends to the lane then almost immediately goes left through trees to pass in front of a corrugated-iron bungalow. Keep straight on, passing a large pond to join a track – the same one that brought you to the Green in the first place.

Turn right into Merrington, a quiet hamlet where Percy Thrower, one of Britain's best-known gardeners, used to live. Go straight on at a junction, then turn left at the next, towards Webscott and Myddle, noticing the memorial stone by the village pump, commemorating Robert Aglionsby Slaney and his wife Elizabeth, who caused a well to be sunk on this site.

On reaching Merrington Grange turn right over a stile onto a footpath which leads to a pasture. Follow the left-hand hedge to the far corner then turn left along the edge of an arable field. Cross to the other side of the hedge where indicated but continue in the same direction to a stile which leads to a meadow. Go slightly right to meet a hedge corner ahead and follow it uphill. Cross a broken stile and footbridge and just keep going towards Pim Hill, the tree-covered ridge ahead. Step over a low fence (the right of way is actually on the other side of the hedge but is currently obstructed) to enter the woodland and turn left. After a few yards a right fork takes you up the hill and you just keep going until you reach the road. There are good views from the top and Pimhill Farm Shop is a short distance to the right.

Walk 7: Hadnall

Start: The Country Garden Plant Centre, Black Birches, Hadnall. Grid
                reference 507216.

Summary: An effortless walk on good paths and quiet lanes in level,
                peaceful countryside. Land use is a mixture of arable and
                pasture and there are some interesting houses to admire. This
                walk is recommended to keen gardeners especially, as it starts
                at a plant centre specialising in roses and unusual plants.

Length: 4 miles.

Maps: OS Landranger 126, OS Pathfinder 848.

Parking: Cars may be left at the Plant Centre as long as the owners are
                informed.

Trains: Nearest station is Yorton (2 miles).

Buses: Boultons/Fishers/Midland Red/North Shropshire Travel
                510/511/512/513/514 from Shrewsbury, Wem and Whitchurch
                to Hadnall; Monday-Saturday. Midland Red/PMT X64 from
                Shrewsbury and Hanley to Astley (1 mile); Monday-Saturday.

The Tea Shop

*Stable Yard Tea Room, Country Garden Plant Centre, Black
Birches, Hadnall.*

The Plant Centre is in the grounds of Black Birches House, a
building with twelfth-century origins, though the present house
is a splendid seventeenth-century mansion with a mock-Tudor
wing added in 1880. Though the centre specialises in roses, it
also has a good range of unusual plants and over 100 varieties of
organically grown herbs. The former stable yard of the house is
the setting for the tea room, which has both indoor and outdoor
seating. Indoors all is fresh and bright and there's a choice of
soups, sandwiches, cakes, sweet and savoury scones, ice creams
and puddings. The choice of drinks is fairly restricted but there
should be something to suit most tastes. Prices are a little higher

than some but portions are generous. Vegetarians can be catered for but only with advance notice, and the owners stipulate that any children must be well-behaved.

Open: 10am-5pm daily, but may close January and February in 1998. Telephone: 01939 210380.

Hadnall Church

The Walk

Walk down the access track to the lane and turn right. Keep straight on at a junction and as you approach another junction look for a stile in the hedge on your left. Enter an arable field and bear left on a path which is usually reinstated by the farmer. If, however, it's not clear, you should walk almost in line with the overhead telephone cables and aim in the direction of a white house. On your right is an attractive range of timber, brick and sandstone buildings at Smethcote Manor.

Go through a gate into a pasture and follow the left-hand hedge to a wooden gate/stile on the left. Climb over and follow the path across another arable field, again heading towards the white house. To the left of it is imposing red brick Haston Farm, of which you will soon enjoy a better view.

A stile gives access to a meadow which you cross to reach a lane, to the left of the white house. Turn right, then go left after passing the house, on what the OS maps show as a lane, but which is in reality more a delightful sandy track riddled in places with rabbit holes. There's a good view of Haston Farm on the left before the lane crosses the railway and heads towards Hadnall.

At the edge of the village the Shropshire Way crosses the lane and our route is to the left, but first it's worth having a quick look round Hadnall, though there are no buildings of outstanding interest. The church is Norman but was largely rebuilt in the nineteenth century. It contains a monument to the first Viscount Hill, who fought with Wellington at Waterloo. He lived for most of his life at Hardwicke Grange to the north of Hadnall. The house has been demolished but the stables survive and are now used as industrial units.

Returning to the Shropshire Way, follow the right-hand hedge until it turns a corner, then go roughly straight ahead to a stile in a fence. Pass a pond, duck under a hawthorn tree and cross a bridge into another field. Walk diagonally right towards a stile just to the right of a house with two mock-Tudor gables. Pass to the right of the house to meet a track then turn right to a lane. Pass through the gate opposite and go along the edge of a paddock to an iron kissing gate in the corner. Join a green lane and when you come to a junction go to the left to enter a pasture. Pass to the right of a hollow which once contained a pond and go over a stile in the hedge ahead. Cross another pasture to reach Mill Lane and continue ahead, passing a house built of huge sandstone blocks and, just beyond it, the truncated remains of Waterloo Windmill, built by Viscount Hill to celebrate his military exploits.

Bear very slightly right across an arable field to a stile in a fence then go diagonally left across pasture before bearing right through a plantation of young spruce trees. Go through a gate and follow

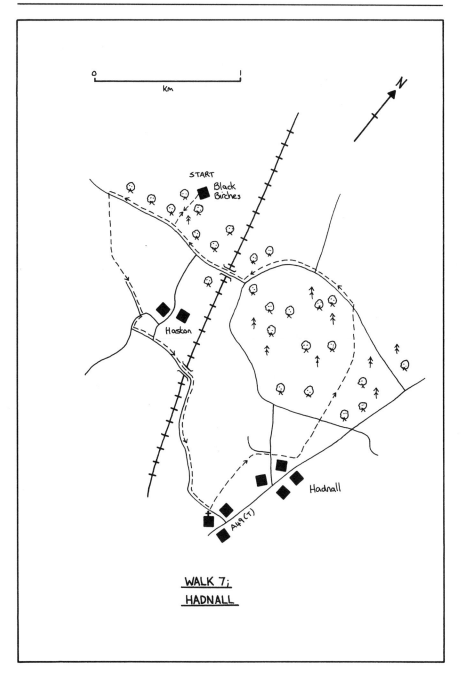

WALK 7;
HADNALL

the path along the edge of woodland surrounding Hardwicke Stables. When you reach a lane there is a good view of Grinshill ahead. Turn left and keep left at a junction. Turn right at the next, passing an interesting range of buildings at Hardwicke Grange Farm as you cross the railway. Go straight on along the lane to return to Black Birches.

Walk 8: Ironbridge

Start: The Iron Bridge, Ironbridge Gorge. Grid reference 673034.

Summary: This was once the most important industrial site in the country but the main feature of this lovely walk is woodland. A visit is also made to Benthall Hall, a National Trust property. There is one gentle climb but it's an easy walk, with only two stiles.

Length: 3½ miles.

Maps: OS Landranger 127, OS Pathfinder 890.

Parking: Public car park south of the Iron Bridge at Ladywood.

Trains: Nearest stations are Telford (5½ miles) and Wellington (7 miles) with frequent bus links.

Buses: Midland Red 6/8/45 from Wellington; daily. Midland Red 9/99 from Bridgnorth; Monday-Saturday. Williamsons/Midland Red/Timeline 96/X96 from Shrewsbury and Birmingham; daily. Elcock Reisen/ Midland Red/Timeline 893/894/895 from Wolverhampton and Wellington; Monday-Saturday.

The Tea Shop

The Ironbridge Gorge Restaurant, The Wharfage, Ironbridge.

This could hardly be more conveniently situated – it's right next door to the tourist information centre and almost opposite the Iron Bridge itself. There's a good choice available, with everything from cream teas to roast lunches. There are hot and cold drinks, including herbal teas and fruit juices, and the accent is on healthy eating. Vegetarians are catered for, dogs are welcome and special meals and a play area are available for children. There is an outside patio at the rear which is attractive in summer. Open: 10am-5pm daily except January. Telephone: 01952 433993.

The Walk

Britain has been an industrial country for many centuries, but on a small scale, with the smelting of iron dependent on wood for fuel. This meant that places where iron ore and woodland coincided became industrial centres – the Sussex Weald, for instance, and the Forest of Dean in Gloucestershire. What changed all that was the discovery by Abraham Darby in 1709 that coke could be used for smelting. Darby's momentous discovery occurred at Coalbrookdale and sparked a revolution which changed the world. Suddenly, iron could be cheaply produced in large quantities, and it was Darby's grandson, Abraham III, who constructed the world's first iron bridge. Cast in 1779, it still spans the Severn just south of Coalbrookdale. The whole area became heavily industrial, only to eventually decline in the face of competition from the Black Country and South Wales. Most of the industrial scars have healed and the Severn Gorge is green once more, but those industrial relics which do survive have been transformed into a collection of museums which offers something of interest for all the family. The Ironbridge Gorge is now a UNESCO-designated World Heritage Site, one of only 14 in Britain.

Ironbridge – from the Iron Bridge

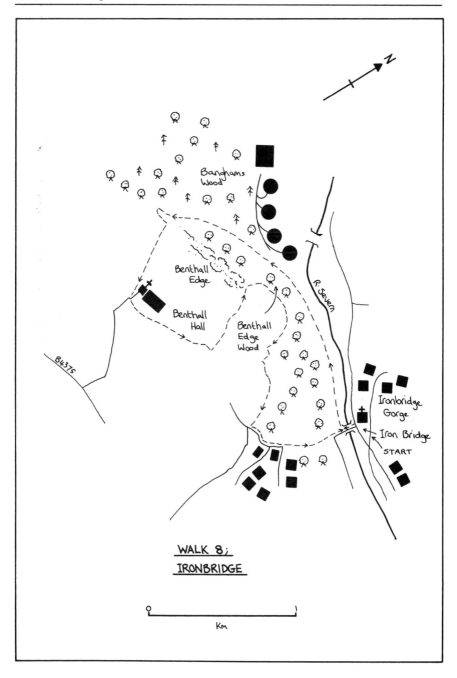

WALK 8;
IRONBRIDGE

Ironbridge itself is built of mellow brick, with attractive buildings clinging in tiers to the north side of the gorge, overlooking
the river. Though it has become a major tourist centre it has not
lost its charm and you can soon escape the crowds by wandering
along the steep, narrow streets well above the congested river
frontage.

The actual Iron Bridge is a graceful structure and the focal point
of the little town. Cross the bridge (if starting in the town) to the
south side of the river to begin the walk, the first stage of which
is through Benthall Edge Wood. This is a delightful place, an area
of dense, almost jungly, broadleaved woodland on a site where,
for centuries, the existing ancient woodland was eaten into by
the demands of industry. Mining and quarrying took place here
from the Middle Ages, but only on a small scale which did
relatively little damage. The Industrial Revolution, however,
meant that brickworks, mines and quarries soon came to domi-
nate the scene, but they are long gone, with only the abandoned,
overgrown workings in the wood to remind us of them. Benthall
Edge Wood today is a combination of patches of ancient woodland which survived the assault of industry, and secondary
woodland which has recolonised the disturbed ground. The
wood is managed by the Severn Gorge Countryside Trust, a
consortium of local authorities and conservation groups. The
Trust allows free public access so you can vary the route described below as much as you wish.

Turn right towards Benthall Edge picnic site then branch left
and shortly left again on the higher of two paths. Fork right at the
next junction and left at the one after. Join the course of the
dismantled Severn Valley Railway. A footpath runs alongside it
on the left – join this at any point you like and follow it through
the wood.

You'll soon see the huge cooling towers of Buildwas power
station ahead. Keep going towards them and you'll come to a
major junction. Two paths lead uphill – take the right-hand one,
an attractive old holloway which climbs steadily. Fork right at
the next junction. The path eventually merges with another

coming in from the right and then bends left, doubling back, and now forming part of the Shropshire Way. Soon after this point, go through a gate on the right, leaving both the wood and the Shropshire Way and joining a green lane which takes you to Benthall.

Pass Benthall Hall Farm and then St Bartholomew's Church. There was originally a Medieval chapel here but it was badly damaged during the Civil War and was rebuilt in 1667. Further alteration took place in the nineteenth century. There are some unusual cast iron headstones in the churchyard and a painted sundial on the church itself. Just beyond the church go into parkland, with Benthall Hall on your left. This imposing house was built in the sixteenth century for William de Benthall. His descendants still live here but the National Trust now owns the property.

Cross to a gate and go on along the left-hand edge of the next field. On reaching a junction turn left and follow a green lane back to Benthall Edge Wood. Turn right, soon rejoining the Shropshire Way. At the second Shropshire Way sign leave it again and turn right. The path soon bends left then wends its way through the trees to the next junction where you fork right. Continuing to another junction, cross a footbridge and climb steps to a T-junction. Turn right, walking between holly trees to find a stile to a field. Turn left along field edges until another stile allows a return to the wood. Turn right into Workhouse Coppice, a Woodland Trust property which takes its name from the former parish workhouse which was situated here. You can explore any of the footpaths in the wood, but for a direct return to Ironbridge go straight on and eventually a gate leads out of the wood, passing the former workhouse (now a private dwelling) to reach a track, Spout Lane, named after a spring which issues from the hillside. Turn left and left again when you reach the road – Bridge Bank – which descends to Ironbridge. Close to the bottom of Bridge Bank, on your right, is the site of a corn mill which was powered by the water from the spout but was dismantled in the 1930s.

Walk 9: Jackfield

Start: Maws Craft Centre, Ferry Road, Jackfield, near Ironbridge. Grid reference 690027.

Summary: An easy walk, partly through residential areas but mainly in woodland, and visiting some fascinating industrial sites. There is one short climb but otherwise it's mainly on level terrain. The walk passes several museum sites which you may wish to visit – if you do, it could easily take all day to complete this short stroll.

Length: 4 miles.

Maps: OS Landranger 127, OS Pathfinder 890.

Parking: At Maws Craft Centre if you're intending to visit the centre and/or the tea shop. It might be as well to confirm permission first. There is a public car park across the river by Coalport High Street.

Trains: Nearest stations are Telford (6½ miles) and Wellington (8 miles) with frequent bus links.

Buses: Williamsons/Midland Red/Timeline 96/X96 from Shrewsbury and Birmingham; daily. Midland Red 9/99 from Bridgnorth and Wellington; Monday-Saturday. Elcock Reisen/Midland Red 895 from Wolverhampton and Wellington; Monday-Saturday. (N.B. some buses call at Coalport or Blists Hill rather than Jackfield).

The Tea Shop

The Painting Shop Tea Room, Maws Craft Centre, Jackfield.

Maws Craft Centre is housed in the surviving buildings of what was once the largest encaustic tileworks in the world. Since taking over the struggling Worcester Tileries in 1850, brothers George and Arthur Maw developed a reputation for quality tiles, many of which are still around today, and sought after by collectors. In 1852 Maws and Company transferred to Benthall to take advantage of local clays, and a rapid expansion culminated in the construction of this factory in 1883. It was closed in 1969 and much of the site demolished, but what remains is worth visiting for its own sake, and also because it houses around twenty craft workshops with a wide variety of items on sale.

The tea shop is bright, colourful, cheerful and altogether enticing. There are displays of old tiles on the walls and prints and crafts for sale. Prices are a little higher than some (though no higher than in tourist-orientated Ironbridge generally) but value for money is undoubted, with generous portions freshly made and beautifully presented. There's a wide choice of soups, snacks, savouries, sandwiches, scones, cakes, jackets, pasta dishes and more besides, and a good range of drinks too. All cakes and meals are homemade and the tea shop has received much praise. Vegetarians are catered for.

Open: 10.30am-5.30pm daily except January. Telephone: 01952 883843.

The Walk

Maws Craft Centre is next to the River Severn and if you stand facing the Severn you'll see the Half Moon Inn on the left. Walk behind it to join a riverside footpath which takes you to Church Road. Pass the church and Jackfield Tile Museum and press on to reach Calcutts Road. Turn left here and soon left again, when you see a footpath sign. The path starts unpromisingly but soon improves. When it forks take the left branch, which leads through woodland. Emerging from the trees by a house, continue in much the same direction on a path opposite, climbing up a wooded bank to reach a track. Turn right to Ironbridge Road and cross to Dark Lane opposite.

The lane climbs towards Broseley, a small town crammed with quietly fascinating buildings missed by most visitors to Ironbridge. Once you've reached the brow of the hill, look out for two large detached houses on the left; between them is a footpath. If you'd like to explore Broseley, carry on along the lane then return to this point later to resume the walk. The path passes old quarry workings before descending through woodland to Ironbridge

Road, forking right as it approaches it. Turn right then cross to
another footpath almost opposite. After passing the entrance to
Coneybury Farm keep straight on along the edge of woodland,
and straight on again at the next junction, following a track which
soon enters another wood, Corbett's Dingle.

Descend through the dingle, with sandstone cliffs on your left
and a brook flashing through a ferny gully on your right. The
ground cover is luxurious, especially in May, when a rampant
tide of wild garlic sweeps through the wood. On leaving the wood
and reaching a house, continue along a track onto a lane then
towards a former railway bridge. Climb the steps to the old
trackbed and turn right on the Severn Valley Way, which eventually descends to the riverbank. A right turn then takes you to
Coalport Bridge, an elegant cast iron structure. The adjacent pub
is called, puzzlingly, The Woodbridge, but the explanation is
simple – the bridge was originally of wood. The present structure
is a mixture of parts made at different times between 1780 and
1818.

Cross the bridge, joining the Silkin Way (a pedestrian/cycleway
using dry canal beds and abandoned railways) which soon turns
left. There is an alternative pedestrian route beside the river.
Either way, you'll soon reach Coalport China Museum, next to
which you'll see a stop lock and a stretch of canal; this is all that
remains of the Coalport section of the Shropshire Canal, which
was once linked to the rest of the Shropshire system. The
Coalport Canal originally had its terminus at a wharf by Coalport
Bridge.

The Shropshire Canal was built by ironmaster William
Reynolds between 1788 and 1792 to link local mines and iron-
works with the Severn. A new town grew up at Coalport and by
1796 the first buildings for the china works were constructed.
When the Coalport branch railway was built the canal suffered
from the competition and ceased operation around 1894. It silted
up and became overgrown but in 1976 the Telford Development
Corporation and the Museum restored this section.

Cross the canal and follow the towpath a short distance to the

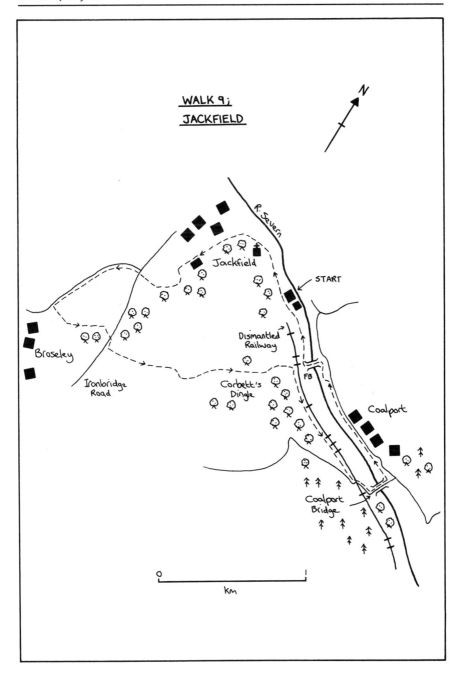

Coalport China Museum

foot of the Hay Inclined Plane. This is one of the country's major industrial monuments and was the means by which boats were transferred between canals. Its completion in 1793 made possible the development of Coalport. Equivalent to 27 locks yet worked by only four men, it could pass a pair of 5-ton tub-boats in four minutes (it would have taken three hours using a lock system). There was no machinery at the bottom; boats were carried up and down the 1 in 3 gradient on wheeled cradles. At first, power was provided by teams of men and horses but eventually an engine was installed at the top of the incline. The site is now part of the Blists Hill Museum. Near the foot of the incline is another fascinating industrial site, the Tar Tunnel (entrance fee) where a spring of natural bitumen was discovered during the digging of a drainage channel.

Cross the footbridge over the River Severn to the Boat Inn. Note the record flood levels marked on the door – the highest being 19ft 5" in February 1946. Turn right, passing the attractive cottages on Ferry Road, to return to Maws Craft Centre.

Walk 10: Much Wenlock

Start: High Street, Much Wenlock. Grid reference 624000.

Summary: A lovely walk, mainly through fields (pasture and arable) but with a scattering of magnificent old oak trees and one delightful wooded section. There are only the gentlest of gradients and route-finding is easy. There are sixteen stiles and one or two marshy patches.

Length: 6½ miles.

Maps: OS Landranger 137, OS Pathfinder 890.

Parking: Public car parks in Much Wenlock, e.g. Back Lane/High Street.

Trains: Nearest stations are Wellington (10 miles) and Telford (10 miles).

Buses: People's Express/Timeline 436/437 from Shrewsbury, Bridgnorth and Kidderminster; Monday-Saturday.

The Tea Shop

The Copper Kettle, 61 High Street, Much Wenlock.

The Copper Kettle occupies the ground floor of a seventeenth-century building which is also the premises of Wenlock Antiques, making a delightful and ideal setting for this popular tea shop. Oak beams, an inglenook with woodburning stove and an array of antique prints on the walls create just the right ambience in which to sample the delicious cakes, pastries and scones on offer. A range of other traditional favourites is available, such as teacakes, toast and sandwiches. More substantial snacks include soups and jacket potatoes. Apart from tea and coffee there are cold drinks and also a choice of ice creams. Prices are very reasonable and all cakes, pastries and soups are homemade. Vegetarians are catered for and service is swift and friendly. Open: 9.30am-5pm except Wednesday (closed) and Sunday (11.30am-5pm). Telephone: 01952 728227.

Wenlock Priory

The Walk

There are plenty of good walks to be had from Much Wenlock, most notably on the escarpment of Wenlock Edge. You'll find no shortage of leaflets and books describing walks on the Edge, but the other countryside around the town is much neglected. This walk is an attempt to redress the balance.

Much Wenlock itself is an immensely picturesque little town, with a wealth of beautiful buildings to admire and it's a good idea to buy a town trail leaflet in the tourist information centre to ensure you don't miss anything of interest. One particularly appealing aspect of Wenlock is the presence of a real working farm in the town centre – Brookhouse Farm, which is of Medieval origin, and is to be found on the corner of Queen Street.

Make your way to the eastern end of the High Street, where The Square is dominated by the timber-framed Guildhall, which dates from 1540. The Town Council still meets here every month. Close by is Holy Trinity Church, founded about AD680 as a place

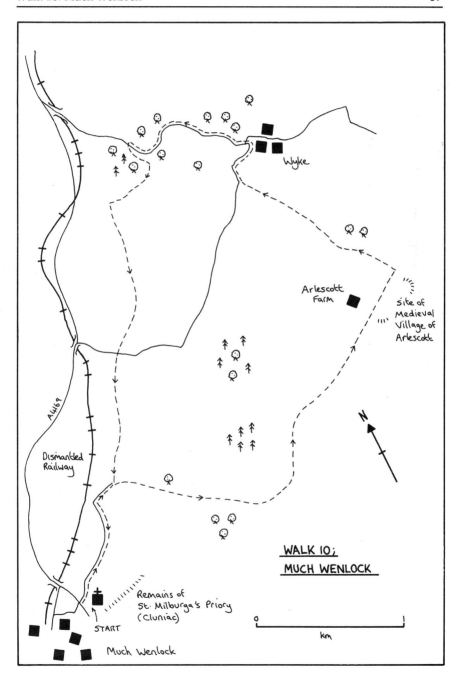

Wyke

Arlescott
Farm

Site of
Medieval
Village of
Arlescott

A4169

Dismantled
Railway

N

WALK 10;
MUCH WENLOCK

Remains of
St· Milburga's Priory
(Cluniac)

START

Much Wenlock

0   1
km

of worship for the nuns of Wenlock Abbey. The church was enlarged between 800 and 1050 and the present nave was built around 1150 by the monks of Wenlock Priory.

Leaving the church, walk along Bull Ring towards Wenlock Priory, an English Heritage property. Although in ruins today, it was once a prosperous and powerful religious centre and a place of pilgrimage. The ruins are those of a Cluniac priory built in the twelfth and thirteenth centuries but the original religious house on this site was founded by Merewalh, a member of the Mercian royal family, during the seventh century.

After visiting the Priory, continue along the lane (also the Shropshire Way), enjoying good views of a low hill surmounted by two areas of woodland – it is around this hill that the walk takes you. On reaching a junction turn right along a track to reach a junction of two footpaths. The Shropshire Way goes left and you will be returning this way later. Now, however, take the path on the right. Cross a brook and follow the left-hand hedge until you draw level with a pond and a waymarked post directs you diagonally across the meadow. Aim first for a short, stout wooden post (it looks like a truncated telegraph pole) then for a stile at the point where the hedge ahead meets a marshy area round a pond.

Once over the stile turn right along the edge of an arable field. When you reach the corner you'll see a gate and stile – ignore both, and turn left along the edge of the field until another stile gives access to the adjacent field. Turn left beside the hedge and walk to the far corner then climb over a low fence and proceed along a narrow path, with a line of trees on your right. Go through a gate at the end of the field and over a stile ahead then straight on through an area of newly planted native trees.

Emerging into a large arable field, keep straight on by the left-hand hedge, enjoying good views of the Wrekin on one side and Brown Clee on the other. Join a track which runs to the left of a holly hedge and when the track bends right, keep straight on across an arable field towards the substantial range of buildings at Arlescott Farm.

Two stiles give access to a sheep pasture to the right of the farm. Turn left across it, aiming towards a cottage. The field is uneven underfoot and there are some obvious earthworks on the right which indicate the site of the deserted Medieval village of Arlescott. Pass to the left of a pool where a spring bubbles to the surface and then to the right of the cottage to intercept the Jack Mytton Way. Turn left to enter a pasture, at which point there's a lovely view ahead, with a shapely oak tree in the foreground and rolling wooded hills beyond, the Wrekin prominent amongst them. The field itself is marked with the ridge and furrow pattern which indicates it was once subject to the plough. When the ridge and furrow ends there are pronounced terraces – these are cultivation terraces, or lynchets, also the result of Celtic or Medieval ploughing.

Just after you pass the terraces, start to veer left away from the hedge to find a waymarked gap in a lower hedge. Turn right and stay on the bridleway until you reach a lane at Wyke below two groups of substantial farm buildings. Turn right and climb up towards the two farms then go left at a road junction, passing a small timber-framed cottage with a massive stone chimney stack, characteristic of many in the area.

You're now back on the Shropshire Way and this is a particularly delightful part of the walk, with woodland crowding in on this quiet lane from both sides. There are deer in the woods and they often venture out to graze by the edges of the lane – go quietly if you hope to see them.

You'll very soon pass the unusual and attractive Tickwood Lodge, and a little further on Tickwood Hall comes into view, a splendid brick house in a fine setting, though sadly the overall effect is rather spoilt by the intrusion of Buildwas power station into the scene. In front of the hall is a field, known as Audience Meadow since 1642 when Charles I met local landowners there to ask for financial help.

All too soon the Shropshire Way makes a left turn off the lane and leads through woodland to open fields. As you pass Woodhouse Farm you may encounter an aggressive dog, but it wants only to escort you off its territory and is soon left behind. The path is clearly waymarked along field edges until you come to a point where the yellow arrow points one way and the buzzard another: the OS map indicates that you walk straight ahead by the left-hand hedge for 250 metres then go diagonally towards Bradley Farm. Pass through the farmyard to turn left by the house and then right. The path crosses a lane and again takes to the fields, going straight ahead until it enters pastureland. At this point bear right to the far right corner, cross a footbridge and turn left past a house. Walk along the drive to rejoin your outward route from Much Wenlock and retrace your steps into town.

Walk 11: Bridgnorth and Astley Abbotts

Start: High Street, High Town, Bridgnorth. Grid reference 716932.

Summary: An easy, level walk in peaceful countryside with a long riverside stretch rich in birdlife. The return leg takes you along the delightful, wooded valley of Cantern Brook, which runs right into Bridgnorth and is very popular with local people. There are 21 stiles.

Length: 7½ miles.

Maps: OS Landranger 138, OS Pathfinder 911.

Parking: Public car parks in Bridgnorth, e.g. Listley Street.

Trains: Nearest mainline station is Telford (12 miles) but the terminus of the Severn Valley Railway is in Bridgnorth, with mainline connections at Kidderminster.

Buses: Midland Red West/People's Express/Timeline/Boulton's/Premier Coaches 297/436/437 from Much Wenlock, Kidderminster and Shrewsbury; Monday-Saturday. Midland Red 890 from Wolverhampton; Monday-Saturday.

The Tea Shop

Beryl's Pantry, Newmarket Buildings, Postern Gate, Bridgnorth.

You'll find Beryl's on the first floor of Newmarket Buildings at the southern end of the High Street. It adjoins the Costume and Childhood Museum, a fascinating glimpse into the social history of Bridgnorth over the last hundred years. Beryl's is a cosy, welcoming, traditional tea room where the service is friendly and everything, except bread, is freshly made on the premises. There's a good range of cakes, scones, sandwiches, salads, soups and snacks. Pots of tea come complete with extra hot water and there are free refills for those ordering coffee. Vegetarians are catered for. A high chair is available for very young children. Homemade preserves and local honey are on sale.

Open: 9am-6pm daily. Telephone: 01746 768550.

The Walk

Bridgnorth always comes as a surprise to those seeing it for the first time because it perches on top of a cliff, in the way of so

Bridgnorth – High Town and St Leonard's Church from the bridge

many continental towns, but so few British ones. It's really two towns – High Town crowns the sandstone cliff, clings to its sides and just gains a foothold on the west bank of the River Severn, while Low Town occupies the east bank of the river. The two are linked by a bridge and a road, with further pedestrian access from the top of High Town to the bridge provided by seven ancient stairways and a cartway cut into the sandstone. A remarkable cliff railway provides an alternative route.

Walk north along High Street, which is lined with many attractive frontages. Most immediately striking is the Town Hall, which occupies a position right in the middle of the road. Built

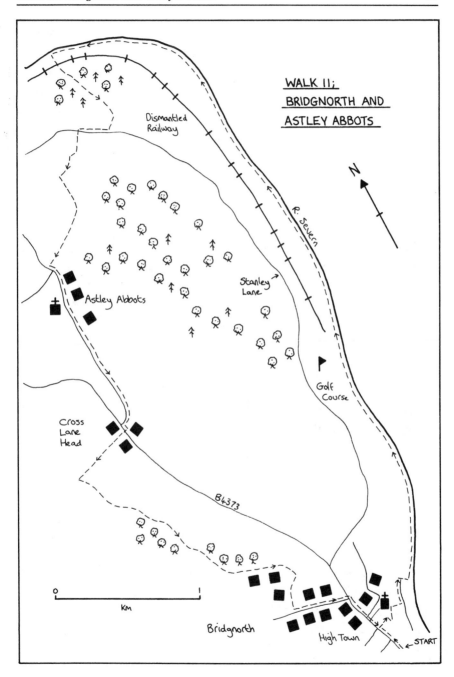

WALK 11;
BRIDGNORTH AND
ASTLEY ABBOTS

N

Dismantled
Railway

R. Severn

Stanley
Lane

Astley Abbots

Golf
Course

Cross
Lane
Head

B4373

0 1

Km

Bridgnorth

High Town

START

in 1648-52 it has a timber upper storey supported by an arched ground floor, built of stone but faced with brick.

At the far end of High Street is Northgate, built in 1740 but rather unappealingly rebuilt in 1910. Just before you reach it turn right down Church Street towards the tall tower of St Leonard's Church. This was the parish church until replaced by Telford's eighteenth-century St Mary's Church, which stands at the other end of town. St Leonard's is now cared for by the Redundant Churches Fund. Though it is almost entirely Victorian it is a commanding edifice of dark red sandstone which stands in a calm little oasis of pleasant period buildings. It was very nearly destroyed by a fire which swept through High Town during the Civil War, but it was expertly repaired, only to fall into dereliction by the nineteenth century when it had to be largely rebuilt. Go down Granary Steps and at the bottom turn left past Granary Cottage. Follow Friars Street to the riverside and turn left. Walk beside the River Severn for the next three miles. Kingfishers and grey wagtails frequent the river and cormorants are present in winter. On the far bank rise pine-clad red sandstone cliffs stained green with mosses and lichens. On your left is the course of the former Severn Valley Railway, which survives south of Bridgnorth but was dismantled to the north of the town. The old railway comes almost to the river bank as you reach a wood, Chestnut Coppice. A stile near this point indicates a footpath to the left but stay by the river for a further quarter mile then join a footpath at a stile by an old gate.

Cross the former railway then walk up the wooded slope opposite, soon turning left at a T-junction. Keep straight on through the plantation then continue along the edge of a field to a lane. Turn right, then left at a sign for Boldings Pools. Pass the entrance to a farmhouse and turn right through the yard, then left. After passing a fishing pool, fork right. Pass between two more pools then go straight on along a wide track across a field.

After 300 metres turn right beside a line of spruce. Go over a stile and turn left along a field edge to reach a lane. Turn left into Astley Abbotts, a small village which once belonged to Shrewsbury Abbey, hence the name. The church, consecrated in 1138, is dedicated to St Calixtus, a slave who became Bishop of Rome in 219. Not much remains of the original church which was rebuilt in 1633 and 1857. It does contain a most unusual relic – a "maiden's garland". These were made for the funerals of unmarried girls and comprise paper flowers attached to a linen-covered wooden frame. This one belonged to Hannah Phillips, drowned crossing the Severn on the eve of her wedding in 1707. There's an unusual headstone in the churchyard too – in memory of John Phillips, killed by a lion from a travelling menagerie.

Another feature of Astley Abbotts is a lavender farm, a rarity in this part of England. You'll see a field of this pretty, fragrant plant next to the church. The farm is open to the public for about a month from the middle of July each year.

Walk on along the lane to reach the main road and cross to a bridleway opposite. As you approach a house, go through a gateway then over a stile on the left. Cross a field to a footbridge then go diagonally right across another field to a footbridge in the corner. Continue beside Cantern Brook, soon entering woodland. The path is undulating and slippery when wet.

Eventually you'll cross a tributary stream at a point where there are two footbridges just yards apart. Go over a stile and turn right up a grassy slope, keeping to the woodland edge. Emerge at Greenfields Court and cross to go up steps opposite and along a passageway to Innage Crescent. Go straight on to a junction and turn left. Just after you pass the fire station you'll see a footbridge giving pedestrian access to the town centre.

Walk 12: Bridgnorth and Rindleford

Start: Severn Bridge, Low Town, Bridgnorth. Grid reference 719930.

Summary: A short, easy walk with just one steep, but very brief, climb near the start. There are only a couple of stiles. Rindleford and The Batch are utterly delightful, more than compensating for some less than exciting arable countryside encountered a little further on. Before the descent back to Bridgnorth a visit is made to a cave system once occupied by hermits.

Length: 6½ miles.

Maps: OS Landranger 138, OS Pathfinder 911.

Parking: Public car parks in Low Town, e.g. St John Street/Severn St. Alternatively, it may be possible to use the car park of the People's Hall Evangelical Church but it is essential to first obtain permission at the tea shop.

Trains: Nearest mainline station is Telford (12 miles) but Bridgnorth is the terminus of the Severn Valley Railway, with mainline connections at Kidderminster.

Buses: Midland Red 9/99 from Wellington; Monday-Saturday. Go Whittle 125 from Kidderminster; Monday-Saturday. Go Whittle 131/132/141/142 from Cleobury Mortimer/Ludlow; Monday-Saturday. Midland Red West/People's Express/Timeline/Boulton's/Premier Coaches 297/436/437 from Much Wenlock, Kidderminster and Shrewsbury; Monday-Saturday. Midland Red 890 from Wolverhampton; Monday-Saturday.

The Tea Shop

The Coffee Pot, 6 St John Street, Low Town, Bridgnorth.

The Coffee Pot is an unusual tea shop in that it's owned by the People's Hall Evangelical Church. A proportion of the profits made is directed towards missionary activity and also back into the local community. It's a small, friendly place with a low, beamed ceiling and a display of old plates on the walls. The prices are low and the menu includes pizza, jacket potatoes and quiche, as well as all the traditional favourites. Soup and a good range of sandwiches are also available. Manageress Julie Dixon is vegetarian so this is one tea shop where the concept is fully understood and veggies can be confident that all the stocks, fats, eggs and cheeses used are suitable. There are crafts, gifts and books for sale. Dogs are welcome if small and well-behaved.

Open: 10am-4pm Monday-Saturday except Tuesday (10am-2pm). Telephone: 01746 768909.

The Cliff Railway at Bridgnorth

The Walk

Low Town is neglected by visitors to Bridgnorth, but it's full of interest in its own right, with many charming buildings, and it also provides a good view of High Town from the bridge which spans the Severn. A notable event which took place just upstream was the construction of the world's first passenger steam locomotive by John Rastrick at Hazledine's Foundry in 1808, to the design of Richard Trevithick.

Don't cross the bridge towards High Town but join the riverside path on the east bank. Walk north through Severn Park until forced to join the main road. Cross with care to a footway opposite and continue northwards for just over a quarter of a mile, with the steep sandstone cliffs of High Rock and Pendlestone Rock on your right.

Look out for bizarre Fort Pendlestone on your left, about a mile from the start of the walk. There is known to have been a corn mill on this site in 1225 and a later building was leased by Abraham Darby in 1760 for iron smelting. In the early part of the nineteenth century it was used as a spinning mill until it burnt down. It was rebuilt by a local landowner and since then has served as a mill, a milk collecting centre, a boat building yard and an industrial estate.

Just after passing the fort join a footpath which climbs steeply up through the lovely woodland clothing Pendlestone Rock. At the top turn left and stay with the path as it swings round to join a green lane. Follow this to a surfaced lane and cross to a footpath on the right. Walk along a field edge until a waymarker directs you to the far right corner of the field. Go through a gate into another field and walk forward a few metres before turning sharp left along the bottom of a small valley, or batch, to use the local word. A stile at the far side gives access to a brackeny area, across which leads a clear path to intercept a track which runs the length of a beautiful wooded valley, simply called The Batch. Turn right along this narrow, steeply enclosed valley and keep straight on at a junction. All too soon the batch meets a more open valley, that of the River Worfe, just as lovely in its own way. Our onward route is to the right but first it's worth a short detour to the left to explore the secluded hamlet of Rindleford a couple of hundred metres away. The main building here is a disused mill, next to which cluster farm buildings, a cottage and a Georgian house, all of them largely unspoilt.

Resuming the walk, follow the river on a sandy track which soon swings right then climbs gently out of the valley. When you reach a lane turn right and walk for nearly half a mile until a

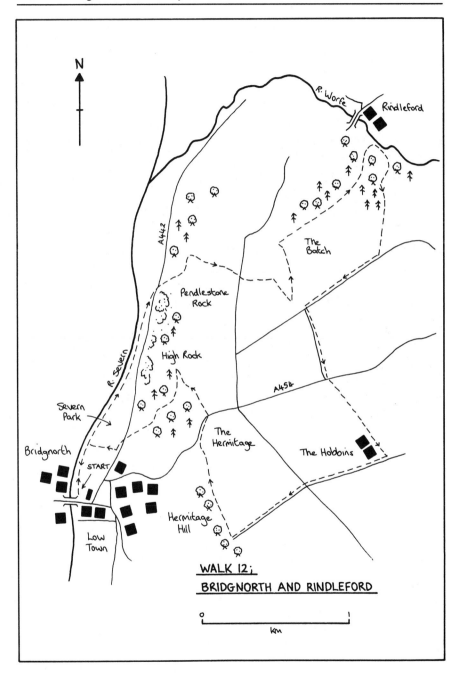

WALK 12;
BRIDGNORTH AND RINDLEFORD

signpost on the left indicates a footpath along the edge of a raspberry field. This leads to a road where the footpath continues opposite, leading past a housing estate called The Hobbins to reach another road.

Turn right along here, perhaps taking the opportunity to explore some of the country park on your left, created on the site of a former RAF training camp. On reaching a road junction, cross to a footpath opposite by Hermitage Farm. The surfaced path runs straight to the top of a bank, Hermitage Hill, where you turn right through a strip of woodland. (Don't follow the surfaced path as it bends right – your footpath is further on, within the wood).

As you approach the main road descend to a lower path to visit the Hermitage, a series of caves gouged out of the sandstone. One local legend has it that each was inhabited by a witch but another tells of occupation in 925 by a hermit Ethelred or Ethelward, a grandson of Alfred the Great. The caves continued in use over the centuries, with the last resident leaving in 1928.

Walk to the road and cross to a footpath opposite which runs along the top of High Rock. After about a quarter of a mile take a path on the left which descends steeply through woodland then levels out as it passes between a cemetery and a pine-topped knoll. It then steepens again as it bends left to descend between the cemetery and a wood. At the bottom turn right to the main road then left. Cross to Severn Park and follow the river to Low Town.

```
┌─────────────────────────────────────────────┐
│                                             │
│        Walk 13: Bridgnorth and              │
│             Eardington                      │
│                                             │
└─────────────────────────────────────────────┘
```

Start: Top of Cartway, High Town, Bridgnorth. Grid reference 717931.

Summary: An easy walk, though with 17 stiles to cross, on good paths and quiet lanes. It includes a stretch of the River Severn before climbing out of the valley to return across pleasant farmland, mainly sheep pasture.

Length: 5 miles.

Maps: OS Landranger 138, OS Pathfinder 911.

Parking: Public car parks in Bridgnorth, e.g. Listley Street.

Trains: Nearest mainline station is Telford (12 miles) but Bridgnorth is the terminus of the Severn Valley Railway, with mainline connections at Kidderminster.

Buses: Midland Red 9/99 from Wellington; Monday-Saturday. Go Whittle 125 from Kidderminster; Monday-Saturday. Go Whittle 131/132/141/142 from Cleobury Mortimer/Ludlow; Monday-Saturday. Midland Red West/People's Express/Timeline/Boulton's/Premier Coaches 297/436/437 from Much Wenlock, Kidderminster and Shrewsbury; Monday-Saturday. Midland Red 890 from Wolverhampton; Monday-Saturday.

The Tea Shop

Dingles Nook Tea Room, 45 Cartway, Bridgnorth.

Dingles Nook sits at the bottom of Cartway, one of the main routes between High Town and Low Town. Behind it is the River Severn and there is an enclosed patio garden which is pleasant in summer. Inside it's small, cosy and warm with a beamed ceiling. Service is prompt and friendly and there are magazines to read. The menu is varied, with all the usual favourites and also a range of more substantial lunches, such as grills, jacket potatoes, lasagne etc. Vegetarians are catered for to some extent, though vegetarian cheese isn't used. Dogs are welcome. Open: 11am(ish)-5pm daily. Telephone: 01746 767231.

The Walk

Cartway is one of the ancient passageways linking the cliff-top
with the riverside and Low Town. You'll find it at the southern
end of High Street, opposite Listley Street. Close by are some of
Bridgnorth's finest and most interesting streets, such as East
Castle Street and Waterloo Terrace. Notice the old street signs
and name plates, an appealing feature of this part of town. It's
worth walking along Castle Terrace to see the cliff railway and
admire the view upriver. Charles I called this the finest view in
his kingdom. He obviously hadn't been up Snowdon . . . But it is
a fine view. The castle dates back to pre-Conquest times and was
rebuilt in stone by Robert de Belesme in 1098-1101. Only the keep
survives and is renowned for having leaned at an angle of 17°
(three times that of the Leaning Tower of Pisa) since slighted by
the Parliamentarians in 1646. Close by is the classical-style
Church of St Mary Magdalene, built to the design of Thomas
Telford in 1792.

Walk down Cartway, which was for centuries the main route
out of Bridgnorth. It led down to a wharf on the Severn which
was in constant use in the days when most trade goods were
carried by boat and the Severn was the second busiest waterway
in Europe. Cartway is lined with lovely buildings, most notable
of which is the timber-framed, gabled Bishop Percy's House,
dated 1580. Notice how some of the houses have heavy wooden
shutters – these were designed for protection from the jostling of
carts, wagons and horses. There are several caves in the sandstone, which were used as homes until the 1850s. At the bottom
of Cartway, join the footpath, part of the Severn Way, which leads
south beside the river. On your right, across the road, are more
caves carved out of the rock.

The well-trodden riverside path is bordered by woodland
which includes alders and willows – trees which are tolerant of
flooding. A great many birds make their home in these woods and
there are also water birds to be seen, including mallards, swans,
kingfishers and herons.

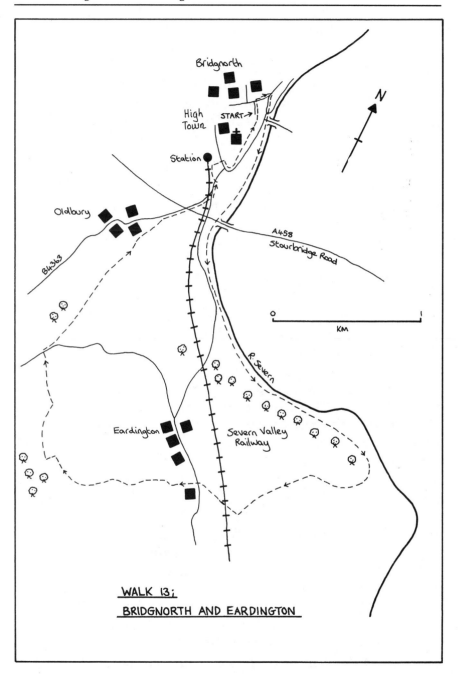

WALK 13;
BRIDGNORTH AND EARDINGTON

After a little over a mile you'll find yourself walking along the base of a steep sandstone cliff, to which further woodland clings, while many more trees, including native wild cherries, have been planted in recent years at the foot of the cliffs.

After passing an abandoned quarry where there are some large beech trees, you enter an arable field. Fork right here, moving away from the river and walking along the bottom of the cliff, which soon gives way to a gentler slope, covered with hawthorn scrub. Keep just to the left of it, beside a fence. As you approach a sewage works, cross a stile on the right and walk up a shallow dry valley which runs through a sheep pasture. There are groves of Scots pines on your right and when you come to the end of these walk to the top left corner of the pasture to join a sandy track.

Continue along this for about half a mile until you see a row of poplars on the right, and a cottage. Turn right beside the trees, cross the Severn Valley Railway by the cottage and follow a track to a road at the small settlement of Eardington.

Turn right beside the road for a few metres then cross to a lane on the other side. Follow this past some impressive houses, including Manor Farm, and just keep going, ignoring any foot-paths which branch off. Notice the unusually wide, dense hedges which border the lane. These contain a good range of species, including elm, elder, field maple, plum, holly, honeysuckle and ivy, as well as the ubiquitous hawthorn.

Quite soon after you pass a farm the lane becomes a green track which leads into a wood. Just before you enter the wood a footpath crosses the lane and there is a stile either side. Cross the one on the right and walk by the woodland edge until it comes to an end and Bridgnorth comes into view ahead. Go diagonally right towards a stile in a hedge a little to the left of an old oak tree. Walk along the right-hand edge of a paddock then just keep going until you meet a tarmac lane. Turn right for a few dozen metres then cross a stile into a field. Take care – this, and subsequent stiles, are armed with barbed wire.

Go diagonally right to a stile in the bottom corner of the field,

One of the many steam locomotives operated by the Severn Valley Railway

cross a brook and enter an arable field. Join a clear, well-trodden path which crosses the field to a stile, then follow a line of trees to another stile. Join a track and keep straight on at all junctions to join a road into Bridgnorth. Turn right and, after passing under the railway, look for steps which take you up to the station, the headquarters of the Severn Valley Railway. There are usually steam or diesel trains by the platform, even if services aren't actually in operation, and there are plenty more in the engine sheds. A footbridge spans the road to the town centre and brings you out near the ruins of the castle.

Walk 14: Billingsley

Start: Rays Farm, Billingsley, Highley, near Bridnorth. Grid reference 714833.

Summary: An easy walk, mainly in woodland but with a small amount of lane-walking. There are about a dozen stiles and you may have to climb over a couple of padlocked gates. There are fine views, an interesting church at Highley and the chance to visit Rays Farm – especially recommended for young children.

Length: 5½ miles.

Maps: OS Landranger 138, OS Pathfinder 932.

Parking: Walkers may leave their cars at Rays Farm – no need to ask permission and no charge if you're going to patronise the tearoom (otherwise 50 pence).

Trains: Nearest mainline station is Kidderminster (10 miles) but there is a Severn Valley Railway station at Highley, with mainline connections at Kidderminster.

Buses: Go Whittle 125 from Kidderminster and Bridgnorth; Monday-Saturday.

The Tea Shop

Rays Farm Country Matters Tea Shop, Billingsley, Highley.

Rays Farm belongs, not to Ray, but to Rose and Frank Cartwright, who opened it as a visitor attraction in 1991. You don't have to pay the entrance fee if you're visiting just the tea shop, which is situated in the former Jersey cow feed room. It's comfortable, reasonably priced and friendly, and there's a good range of homemade scones, cakes and pastries, freshly baked daily. Sandwiches and snacks on toast are on the menu too, and vegetarians are catered for. Maps of short walks starting at Rays Farm are available for a small charge which goes towards supporting two local churches. There are gifts on sale too, ranging fron locally made preserves to some unusual string puppets.

Open: 10am-6pm daily 1st March to 24th December; 10am-dusk weekends and school holidays 27th December-28th February. Telephone: 01299 841255.

The Walk

Rays Farm takes its name from the local area, which is known as The Rays. Opinion is divided as to whether the name is French or Anglo-Saxon in origin. Parts of the farm itself may date back as far as 1500 and it used to be devoted mainly to rearing cattle. Today it's purely a visitor attraction in a lovely setting. Most of the animals on display are traditional British farm breeds, with some notable exceptions, such as Sebastian the llama. There are also deer, peafowl and owls.

Leaving the farm, turn right along the lane (also the Jack Mytton Way). On reaching a T-junction turn left then almost immediately join a bridleway which follows a well-trodden route through woodland, keeping close to a brook. When you reach a gate go into a field and turn right, climbing slightly through scrub then continuing along a narrow strip of pasture towards a farm. Follow the waymarked route round it to join the farm access track at a cattle grid. Walk along the track until it bends left. Continue straight on instead, across pasture with a hedge on your right. When the hedge turns a corner carry straight on across the field, towards a white-painted pub with a tall chimney. A stile gives access to the road, where you turn right, and then left, on a lane signposted to New England and Highley.

The lane takes a ridge-top route before eventually descending steeply to a ford, which may be avoided by taking a path on the right leading to a footbridge.

Continue along the lane, climbing out of the valley, to join the second footpath on the right, after about a quarter of a mile. Bear slightly left across an arable field towards a hedge corner, go through a gap and continue along the edge of the next field to reach a golf course. An avenue of young trees defines the route across the first part of the course to a track, where you go left to join another avenue of trees.

Climb a stile to a lane and join a footpath opposite. Go straight on to a junction, turn right then soon left. Turn right at a T-junction, shortly joining a footpath which leads past houses. Go diagonally across a field to a stile then turn left to reach the High Street at Highley.

Shropshire has many picturesque villages; Highley, sadly, isn't one of them. It is a settlement of great antiquity, however, which probably originated as a clearing in Wyre Forest. It has long been associated with industry, especially quarrying, which took place close to the river. Coal-mining began about 1800 but didn't become established until the end of the 1870s and didn't reach its peak until 1957, when Highley Colliery was employing 1000 men. It closed in 1967 and since then the colliery site has been transformed into the Severn Valley Country Park, which straddles the river. A footbridge, formerly used by the miners, connects the west bank with the east, where Alveley was also a mining village. Thousands of trees have been planted and the

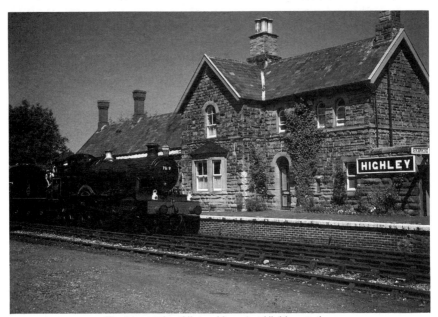

The locomotive 'Hinton Manor' at Highley station

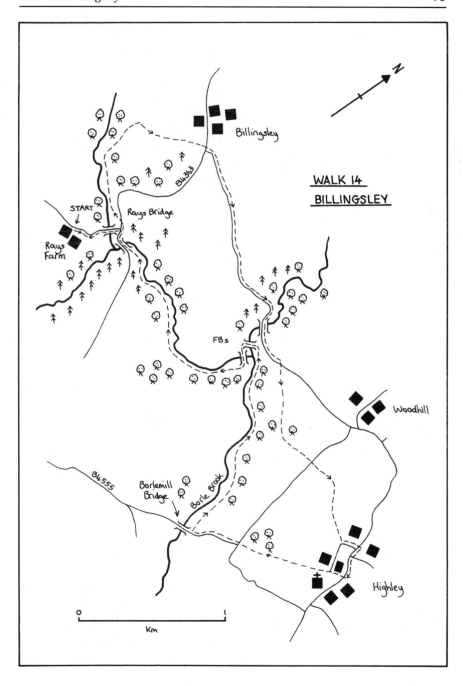

industrial scars have healed. The Severn Valley Railway runs through the park, beside the river, and Highley station is beautifully kept.

Turn right along the High Street and walk to the church, next to which stands timber-framed Church House. The two together constitute by far the most picturesque corner of the village. A late Medieval building, Church House was the home of the village priest until the 1620s. St Mary's Church was first mentioned in a mid-twelfth-century document, and much of the present nave and chancel probably date from this period.

Walk past Church House and continue past a farm to find a stile in a hedge ahead. Go straight on over pastureland to reach Netherton Lane. Walk down another lane opposite, signposted to Borle Mill and Kinlet. A steep descent leads to Borle Brook, but just before you reach it join the first footpath on the right, which runs past Borle Mill and keeps to the east of the brook, soon entering woodland.

The valleys of Borle Brook and its tributaries are mostly wooded, with oak and ash the dominant species in the drier areas. Close to the brook more water-tolerant species occur, predominantly willow and alder. The woods were formerly coppiced and the woodland canopy shades a variety of wild flowers. A tramway (it's now a footpath) used to run along the other side of the brook, joining a colliery at Billingsley to a wharf at Brooksmouth on the Severn. The colliery closed in 1921, though the railway remained operative for a time to serve a coal wharf at Billingsley.

As you progress through the wood keep a sharp lookout for a trodden-down barbed wire fence across the path at one point, which could easily cause a fall. After a little over three-quarters of a mile a path descends left to Donkey Bridge. One local tradition has it that this was a packhorse bridge, but another maintains that it was built in 1708 by the Squire of Kinlet, Sir William Childe. It is shown on a map of 1756 as New Bridge.

Cross the bridge and turn left, climbing slightly to a junction of three paths. Take the middle one, the widest of the three, which is part of the Jack Mytton Way. Turn left again at an old railway bridge, joining the route of the tramway which ran to Billingsley. The path takes you through woodland to the left of Scotts Brook. When you reach the road at Rays Bridge you're at the site which housed the coal preparation plant (the screens). The colliery itself was high on the hill above and coal was sent down an incline. After the mine closed a coal wharf was built on the site of the screens. Turn right, then left, to return to Rays Farm.

Walk 15: Cleobury Mortimer

Start: Lion Lane, Cleobury Mortimer. Grid reference 674757.

Summary: A short, undemanding walk, mostly on well-defined paths and with only the gentlest of slopes. It combines pasture, woodland and parkland with an attractive stretch of the River Rea. There are six stiles.

Length: 3½ miles.

Maps: OS Landranger 138, OS Pathfinder 952.

Parking: Public car park on Childe Road.

Trains: Nearest stations are Kidderminster (11 miles) and Ludlow (11 miles).

Buses: Midland Red West/Go Whittle 192/292 from Birmingham, Kidderminster, Ludlow and Hereford; daily.

The Tea Shop

Rest-a-While, 6 Church Street, Cleobury Mortimer.

Rest-a-While occupies a corner of a shop selling cards and artists' materials, situated on the corner of Church Street and Lion Lane opposite the church. It has attractive wood-panelled walls and exposed ceiling beams and provides a good range of snacks and lunches, everything from scones and teacakes to lasagne and curry. The usual variety of hot and cold drinks is on offer and you can have free refills of tea or coffee if you accompany your drink with a meal. Dogs are welcome. Open: 9.30am-5pm Monday-Saturday. Telephone: 01299 271460.

The Walk

Seen from a distance, Cleobury (pronounced Clibbury) Mortimer is instantly recognisable, thanks to the crooked spire of St Mary's Church, which owes this characteristic to the warping of its

Cleobury Mortimer

timbers. Built of a greyish sandstone, St Mary's is mostly of the twelfth and thirteenth centuries, though there are many later alterations and additions. To the north-west of the churchyard is the site of a castle probably built by Ralph Mortimer in the 1150s but destroyed by Henry II soon after. Hugh Mortimer rebuilt it some time before 1179 and made it his chief residence but nothing remains today.

Though Cleobury is often referred to as a town rather than a village, this is more a courtesy title than anything else, though it is the natural centre for quite a large area. There is just one main street but this is lined with attractive buildings in a harmonious mix of sizes and styles, though the emphasis is on the Georgian period. Cleobury is fortunate in its situation, with the Clee Hills providing an impressive backdrop.

The church has a memorial window, made in 1875, to William Langland, the fourteenth-century author of the famous allegorical poem Piers Plowman. Though Cleobury claims to be Langland's birthplace in 1332, the same claim is made, possibly with more justification, by Ledbury in Herefordshire. What is not in dispute is that Cleobury was the home of a more modern poet, Simon Evans, who sought tranquillity here after his experiences in the First World War. He became a postman and completed a nine-mile walk every day to the north of the town, the peace and beauty of the countryside inspiring several volumes of poetry before he died in 1940.

Begin the walk by following Lion Lane. Where it bends sharp left there are two stiles ahead. Take the left-hand one, and climb up a bank. At the top continue in the same direction to pass just to the right of a farm, then keep going to a gate at the far side of a pasture. Ignore a gate to a lane and follow the left-hand edge of the next field before skirting a wooded dingle to reach the lane. Turn right for about 500 metres, climbing steadily to the top of a rise, after which the lane levels out and then descends very slightly. Take an unsigned track on the left which leads to a farm, The Rookery. After passing an attractive range of brick stables there is a good view of Mawley Hall on a hill to your left.

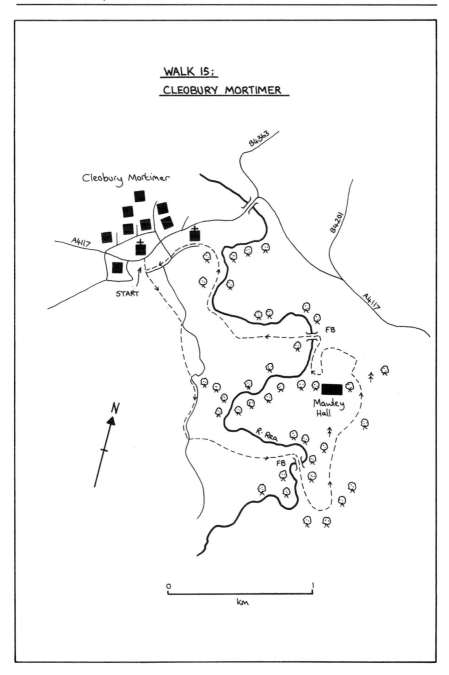

This imposing red brick house was built around 1730 for Sir Edward Blount (pronounced Blunt). The exterior is a model of restraint but the interior is said to be magnificent, the finest of its period in the county. Though not generally open to the public, admission may be granted on written application to the administrator. The architect of Mawley Hall is not known for certain, but is thought to have been Francis Smith of Warwick.

Stay on the track, which leads down to a ford and footbridge next to a weir on the River Rea (pronounced Ree). Though this hardly looks like an industrial site, there was once a charcoal furnace here, built in the sixteenth century for smelting iron ore. Cross the bridge and then another one and turn right beside the river, on the other bank of which (in Worcestershire) is a lovely stretch of woodland, predominantly of oak and birch.

Soon after passing another footbridge the track swings left uphill and away from the river, climbing steadily past a conifer plantation to pass Mawley Hall. Before long it curves left to meet another track where you turn right, then shortly left, to walk round a walled garden and descend to the river again. Follow it to a footbridge and cross over then go straight on up the edge of a field. Continue in the same direction until a waymarker on a gate indicates a footpath on the right. Descend to the river once more and follow it to Cleobury Mortimer, joining a surfaced lane, Pinkham, near an old mill. Stay on Pinkham, which leads directly back to Lion Lane.

Walk 16: Ludlow and Bromfield

Start: Castle Square, Ludlow. Grid reference 510746.

Summary: An easy walk almost entirely on the level and mainly on hard-surfaced tracks and well-defined bridleways. There are no stiles. The pleasant village of Bromfield is explored at the halfway point and Ludlow itself is quite superb.

Length: 5½ miles.

Maps: OS Landranger 137 or 138, OS Pathfinder 951.

Parking: Public car parks in Ludlow, e.g. Lower Galdeford.

Trains: Daily services on the Cardiff-Manchester/Liverpool line.

Buses: Midland Red West/Go Whittle 192/292 from Birmingham, Kidderminster and Hereford; daily. Midland Red 435 from Shrewsbury; Monday-Saturday

The Tea Shop

Castle Lodge Buttery, Castle Square, Ludlow.

Castle Lodge Buttery takes its name from the adjoining Castle Lodge, a house with fourteenth-century origins, though most of what we see today is the result of rebuilding in 1580. Despite the ancient pedigree of its neighbour, Castle Lodge Buttery is not a traditional-style tea shop, but it is warm, welcoming and conveniently situated in the heart of town. It's run by Mrs and Mrs Manley and their daughter Vicki who provide a range of drinks, sandwiches, baguettes, cakes and homemade soup and claim to be "infamous for our hot frothy coffee and delicious hot chocolate." An attempt is made to cater for vegetarians: most of the cakes and scones are made with butter and free range eggs are used. Soups, however, are made with chicken stock. Though dogs are not permitted they may be tied up outside.

Open: 9am-5.30pm Monday-Saturday and 10am-6pm Sunday in summer; 9am-5pm Monday-Saturday in winter. Telephone: 01584 873628.

Ludlow: The Feathers

The Walk

Ludlow is Shropshire's loveliest town, and one of the finest in the country. It's beautifully situated and is crammed with a total of 469 listed buildings. Though it's possible that there was a small Saxon settlement on the site, Ludlow's history really began about 20 years after the Norman Conquest, when Roger de Lacy built a castle on a fine defensive site high above the confluence of the Teme and the Corve. A planned town was laid out in a grid pattern outside the castle gates and was soon a thriving centre. The castle was later greatly extended and town walls were begun in 1233, enclosing the castle within their circuit.

Ludlow grew rich trading in wool and cloth and gained additional importance in 1475 when the castle became the seat of the Council for the Marches and Wales, which was charged with the administration of this often turbulent area. After the Council was abolished in 1689 the castle fell into disuse but the town continued to prosper and became a fashionable social centre for wealthy county families in the eighteenth and nineteenth centuries. Today, Ludlow still thrives as energetically as ever, and is renowned for the superb festival it stages for a fortnight every summer, the highlight of which is the twice-daily performance of a Shakespeare play in the ruined castle.

Stand facing the castle, with Castle Lodge Buttery on your left, and take a footpath on the right which follows the castle walls to a junction. Turn sharp right on another path which descends to a lane, Linney. Follow this as it curves left by a house called Rhosymedre then keep going until the lane turns right. Leave it at this point, going straight ahead on a footpath waymarked with the buzzard logo of the Shropshire Way. (At the time of writing, this footpath is closed to allow repairs to a bridge; if this is still the case simply continue along Linney to the main road then turn left to join Burway Lane.)

The footpath takes you across fields, via two footbridges, to the main road. Turn left, then left again on a bridleway, Burway Lane, still on the Shropshire Way. After passing Burway Farm the bridleway becomes a field edge route which eventually turns sharp right towards the A49.

Turn left along the edge of a field, with the main road just the other side of the hedge. After a little over half a mile you have to join the road but there is a footway and you soon turn left into Bromfield. After a few metres the road bends right – walk along here if you wish to look at the picturesque cottages which constitute the main part of the village; otherwise keep straight on along a bridleway to St Mary's Church.

Despite the noisy presence of the A49 the churchyard is something of an oasis, thanks to the native flowers which are allowed to flourish here. Perhaps most notable are the wild daffodils in February and March, though they're rivalled by the lovely cuckoo flowers which take over in April, attracting the pretty orange-tip butterfly which lays its eggs on their leaves. Another memorable feature of the churchyard is the avenue of 40 yew trees on the eastern side. The church itself, which stands close by the confluence of the Onny and the Teme, has its origins around AD900, though the present building is somewhat later than this. Part of it once formed the chapel of a priory established here in 1135 and affiliated to the Benedictine Abbey of St Peter's at Gloucester in 1155. The priory was dissolved by Henry VIII and all that remains is a stone and half-timbered gatehouse which was built in the fourteenth century.

Returning to the bridleway, follow it through Oakly Park, the estate of the Earl of Plymouth, whose house is passed about half a mile from the church. Just keep straight on, ignoring all turnings, and eventually passing a farm, Priors Halton, after which the bridleway becomes a lane which takes you to Dinham Bridge where you cross the Teme and climb uphill into Ludlow.

On the way you pass what may be Ludlow's oldest building, the remains of a chapel dedicated to St Thomas of Canterbury, built around 1190. More attractive buildings, including the splendid Dinham House, accompany you as you walk up to Castle Square.

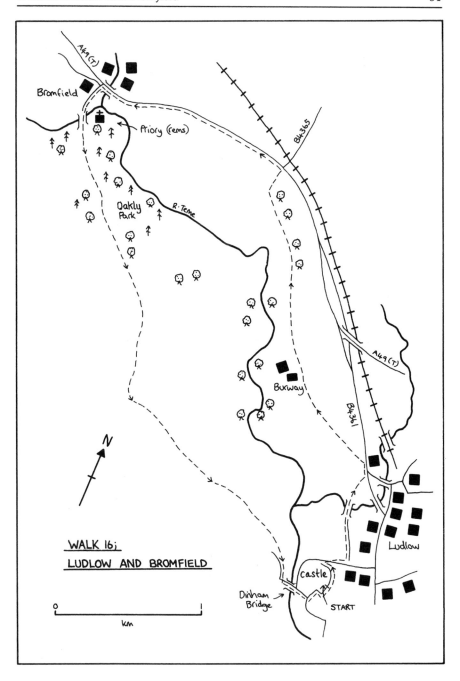

WALK 16;
LUDLOW AND BROMFIELD

Walk 17: Ludlow and Mary Knoll

Start: The Bull Ring, Ludlow. Grid reference 513746.

Summary: A lovely walk which gives a brief taste of the delights of Mortimer Forest. Mainly on well-defined footpaths and bridleways, it includes a gentle but steady climb into the forest. There are very few stiles.

Length: 5½ miles.

Maps: OS Landranger 137 or 138, OS Pathfinder 951.

Parking: Public car parks in Ludlow, e.g. Lower Galdeford.

Trains: Daily services on the Cardiff-Manchester/Liverpool line.

Buses: Midland Red West/Go Whittle 192/292 from Birmingham, Kidderminster and Hereford; daily. Midland Red 435 from Shrewsbury; Monday-Saturday.

The Tea Shop
The Old Bakehouse Restaurant, Tower Street, Ludlow.

Tower Street is just off the Bull Ring, and The Old Bakehouse occupies a building which was formerly Ludlow's oldest bakery. Owner Lisa Brown runs a cosy, traditional tea shop with wooden floors and ceiling beams and an old pine dresser overflowing with a tempting display of homemade cakes. There's a wide range of sandwiches, snacks, salads and soups as well as more substantial meals and a good choice of drinks. Free range eggs are used and vegetarian cheese when available. Most, but not all, soups are made with vegetable stock.
Open: 9am-5pm(ish) Monday-Thursday, 9am-9pm(ish) Friday-Saturday, 10am-6pm(ish) Sunday. Telephone: 01584 872645.

The Walk
The Bull Ring is the area at the top of the hill where the main through road (the B4361 Corve Street/Old Street) intersects

Ludlow and Brown Clee Hill from Whitcliffe

Tower Street and King Street. When Ludlow was first laid out in the eleventh century the market place stretched from the castle to the Bull Ring, but most of this huge area was later filled in with buildings. It's well worth exploring this part of town and certainly every visitor should take the opportunity to visit St Laurence's, the largest and most majestic parish church in Shropshire.

Despite its size, the church is scarcely visible from the town centre, so hemmed in is it by buildings. It's only when you view Ludlow from a distance that St Laurence's real stature is apparent. It dates from the twelfth century but most of what exists today is fifteenth century, and was built with profits from the wool trade. There are many fine monuments and furnishings inside, and a memorial stone to the poet A.E. Housman is to be found on the exterior wall near the north door.

After visiting the church make your way to Castle Square by way of Church Street, High Street or Harp Lane. Turn left by the castle to walk down Dinham. Cross the River Teme by Dinham

Bridge, go through a gap in the wall on the left and up steep steps cut into the cliff which forms part of Whitcliffe Common. You'll notice a series of waymarked posts which indicate you're on the Mortimer Trail.

Whitcliffe is an area of mostly wooded common with plenty of footpaths to explore. A charter of 1241 granted all second generation Ludlovians the right to graze two cows or horses or six sheep on the common and to let their pigs loose on it at acorn time. Today, the people of Ludlow mostly come here to walk their dogs and enjoy the splendid views of their lovely town.

The Mortimer Trail is a 30-mile walking route between Ludlow and Kington(Herefordshire). The same name has been appropriated by the Forestry Commission which lumps together its scattered holdings in North Herefordshire and South Shropshire as Mortimer Forest. Though applied collectively, the name is also used for the individual block of forest on the edge of Ludlow which this walk explores. The historical connection with the Mortimers is real enough, for the land encompassed by this term includes former Saxon hunting forests which were given by William I to Ralph Mortimer after the Conquest. Mortimer, created Earl of March, built a castle at Wigmore and for 300 years his descendants ruled this part of the border country.

Though the emphasis in Mortimer Forest is very much on coniferous woodland, the Commission does manage the paths and rides with wildlife in mind. Broad verges open to the light encourage the growth of flowers, which attract butterflies, and the forest is known for its populations of commas and silver-washed fritillaries. Look out for deer too – Mortimer Forest is home to a unique, long-haired race of fallow deer. Despite much research, nobody is quite sure why they occur here and nowhere else, although it is believed the unique strain evolved after a single gene mutation. Sadly, it is now feared they could face extinction as a result of poaching. The BSE crisis has led to increased demand for venison and evidence that poachers are killing large numbers of deer, probably for the black market, was first discovered in August 1996.

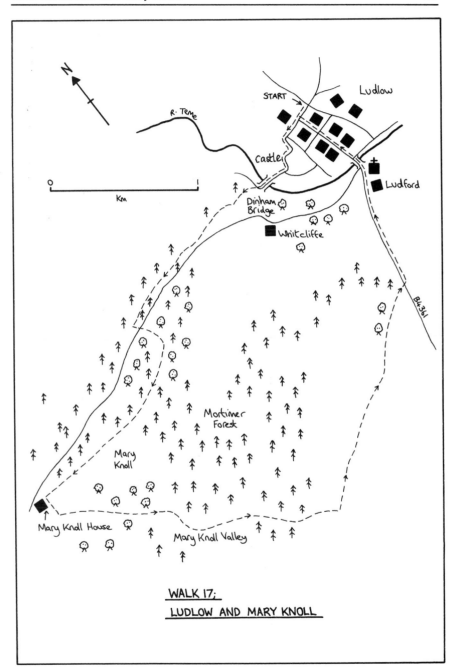

WALK 17;
LUDLOW AND MARY KNOLL

Follow the Mortimer Trail for the next mile or so. It takes you over the common then along a "no through road" to a path which climbs up into Mortimer Forest through woods of chestnut, oak and beech. A stretch of conifers then ensues before the path makes a left turn to a car park by a minor road.

Cross the road and go straight on up the track opposite towards the Forestry Commission's Marches District Office. Keep straight on at a crossroads, still on the Mortimer Trail. At a nine-ways junction turn right, directly opposite a sign for an educational trail, then immediately branch left on a sunken path, leaving the Mortimer Trail behind.

Keep straight on at a junction, so that you're soon walking just below the top of a ridge, Mary Knoll, which coincides with the border between Shropshire and Herefordshire and provides superb views to the north. Pass a barn to reach Mary Knoll House then turn left, going downhill on a bridleway. Fork left at a junction and keep descending. Go through a gate into the forest and shortly fork right, descending steeply to join a track by a stream and follow it down Mary Knoll Valley. On reaching a major junction turn left.

When you come to a junction near a cottage go left past an old quarry. The track climbs gently and as it bends left leave it to go straight on along a bridleway, passing through a deer gate into a hedged lane. Keep going to pass a solitary house, Starvecrow, and continue to a T-junction where you turn left. Walk along the edge of a field then past a garden and down the drive of a house, Mabbitt's Horn, to Overton Road. Turn left to reach Ludford.

This tiny hamlet is missed by most visitors to Ludlow but it's a picturesque place, well worth a closer look. The small cluster of buildings includes a Norman church and an almshouse, St Giles' Hospital, founded in 1216. The Old Bell is a timber-framed house of 1614 which was once a pub and Ludford House is an impressive building which is either late Elizabethan or early Jacobean. Ludford Bridge is a triple-arched structure which dates from the fifteenth century.

Cross the bridge and walk up Lower Broad Street and Broad Street to reach King Street. Turn right to return to the Bull Ring. Broad Street, lined with elegant Georgian houses, is described by Pevsner as "one of the most memorable streets in England" and it's a great pity that it's allowed to be dominated these days by parked cars. The Broad Gate itself, one of seven which once guarded the town walls, still stands, with the addition of an attractive castellated house built over it in the eighteenth century. At the top of Broad Street is the Butter Cross, built of stone in 1743 and originally intended as the Town Hall

---

Walk 18: Onibury

Start: Onibury Station, Onibury. Grid reference 454792.

Summary: An easy and very pleasant walk in gently undulating terrain, mainly pasture but with some woodland and a couple of arable fields. One of its main features is an abundance of superb old trees and hedges. There are about eight stiles and you may have to climb over an electric fence.

Length: 5 miles.

Maps: OS Landranger 137, OS Pathfinders 931 and 951.

Parking: Walkers may leave their cars in the large field next to the station when it's open, but should ask first.

Trains: Nearest station is Craven Arms (2 miles from the Rotting Wood footpath). The 435 bus provides a link from the station.

Buses: Midland Red 435 from Shrewsbury and Ludlow; Monday - Saturday.

The Tea Shop

Onibury Station, Onibury, near Craven Arms.

Sadly, trains no longer stop at Onibury, where the former station house is an attractive stone building, adjoining which is a large garden, in which owner Vivienne Parry serves teas, snacks, meals and 13 varieties of homemade ice cream. There's a summer house and sheltered spots out of the wind for those colder days. Everything is homemade and freshly cooked to order. Vegetarians are catered for to some extent but should ask for details. It's a very friendly, homely sort of place, and a café rather than a traditional tea shop – if you crave chips you can get them here. A wide range of snacks is available, including omelettes, grills and sandwiches. Portions are incredibly generous. Dogs are welcome, but make sure they're under control as Vivienne has two small dogs of her own, and at least one cat. The long opening hours here are a real bonus.

Open: 8am-9pm daily Easter weekend until the second week in October. Telephone: 01584 856336.

The Walk

Situated close to the River Onny, Onibury is a small village with a few attractive cottages in stone and half-timbering. St Michael's Church is a lovely building which dates from the Norman period but also contains work of the thirteenth, fourteenth and fifteenth centuries, though it was restored in 1902. Both Onibury and the River Onny take their name from a Welsh word on(n), which means ash trees, but today there are more oaks than ash. Holly trees are unusually common in the area, a fact reflected in the name of a pub – The Hollybush – which once stood at Onibury. The Ilex Studio continues the tradition – ilex is the Latin for holly.

Walk along the lane into the village, turning right by the Post Office Stores. Pass the church and the Ilex Studio then turn left on the Shropshire Way. After 200 metres climb a stile on the right

Onibury Church

and leave the Shropshire Way, which heads off across the field. Instead, turn left by the hedge. As the footpath climbs gently uphill you enjoy increasingly good views of the Clee Hills, Ludlow and Mortimer Forest. After following the edges of three fields continue across the middle of two more to reach a gate into another. Go diagonally right to cross a bridge near the hollow, horizontal but still living trunk of a huge poplar.

Walk up a long, narrow pasture to a stile on the right. After climbing this go diagonally left over two more pastures towards a cluster of barns ahead. Join a vehicle track and pass between the barns then through a new gate and straight on along the right-hand edge of a field. When you leave the field turn left and follow a clear track to reach a lane.

Turn left and walk to a junction where you turn right between high-banked hedges towards the hamlet of Norton. As you approach the entrance to a farm look for a bridleway sign on the left and join a lovely holloway enclosed by banks of shaly limestone luxuriantly clothed in mosses, ferns and ivy. In wet weather it can be very wet and slippery underfoot.

All too soon a gate leads to a track where you turn right. After about half a mile you come to two gates waymarked with yellow arrows. Go through the left-hand one and keep straight on to the end of a field. Go through a gate on the right and turn left to walk along the outer edge of Rotting Wood. Very soon another gate provides access to the interior of the wood. Uphill on your right dense woodland clothes the ramparts of Norton Camp, an Iron Age fort on a well-chosen site – it must have commanded extensive views over the Onny Valley and beyond.

Descend to a junction by an old quarry then keep straight on through chestnut trees. At a T-junction turn right past a cottage to a waymarked post, then sharp left on an easily missed track which leads to another. Turn left and walk up a slope towards The Rock, forking left just before a sign for Park Croft. Walk up to a lovely cottage guarded by two stone cockerels and turn right on a green track.

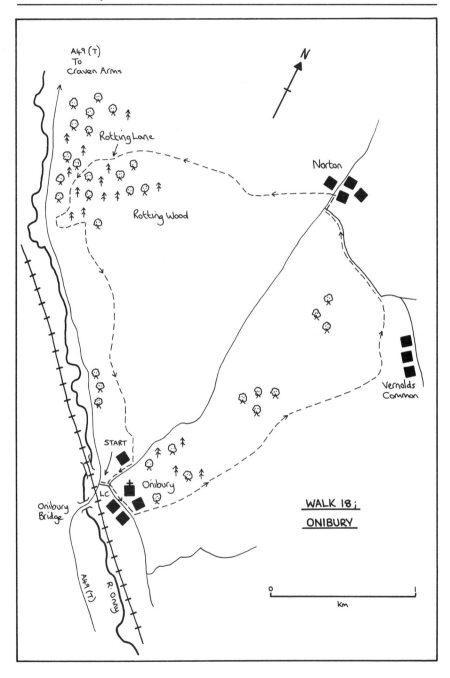

A49 (T)
To
Craven Arms

N

Rotting Lane

Rotting Wood

Norton

START

Onibury

LC

Onibury
Bridge

A49 (T)

R. Onny

Vernolds
Common

WALK 18;
ONIBURY

0   1

km

Go through a gate into a field and follow a sunken path by the right-hand hedge to a bridleway gate. Turn left in front of a converted barn then left again, soon passing between two old Dutch barns. Go through a gate into a field and straight across to a small bridleway gate. Follow a clear path across pasture, trending left to pass through the middle of a group of barns then on along a track. After passing a house turn right, and right again at a lane on the edge of Onibury.

Walk 19: Stokesay Castle

Start: Stokesay Castle, Stokesay, Craven Arms. Grid reference 436817.

Summary: A slightly longer walk but an undemanding one with only the gentlest of slopes. Mainly pasture and woodland, with a total of 18 stiles. It includes some beautiful old green lanes and the almost impossibly picturesque Stokesay Castle.

Length: 8 miles.

Maps: OS Landranger 137, OS Pathfinders 931 and 951.

Parking: Lay-by on the A49 next to the Stokesay turn.

Trains: Nearest station is Craven Arms (1 mile). Daily services on the Cardiff-Manchester/Liverpool line and Swansea-Shrewsbury (Heart of Wales) line. The 435 provides a bus link.

Buses: Midland Red 435 from Shrewsbury and Ludlow; Monday-Saturday.

The Tea Shop

Stokesay Pottery Tea Room, Stokesay, Craven Arms.

The tea room occupies a cottage opposite the castle and has tables outside as well as indoors. There is a fairly limited range of snacks on offer but it includes some delicious cakes and scones and there's a good choice of speciality teas. It's not just a tea room but also an Aladdin's cave bursting with bric-à-brac, books and records. There are local prints on the wall, all for sale, and plants are available too. Best of all, at least one of the four resident tabby cats is likely to welcome you. Although in the past there has been little attempt to cater for vegetarians, this is an issue the proprietors are reconsidering and their soups are now being made with homemade vegetable stock. Dogs are welcome.

Open: 10am-dusk daily April-October; 10am-4pm November-March Wednesday-Sunday only – these times are variable but basically much the same hours are kept as at the castle, except that the tea room is open longer on summer days (the castle closes at 4pm) and will open on demand in winter. Telephone: 01588 673723.

The Walk

Stokesay Castle isn't really a castle at all, but a fortified manor-house. Built in the thirteenth century by a wealthy wool merchant, Laurence of Ludlow, it is the best preserved and probably the oldest example of its kind in England. The timber-framed gatehouse was added later, in the Elizabethan period. The name Stokesay originally meant the stoke (enclosure) of the Norman family de Saye, who owned the site from 1105 until 1255. Laurence bought it in 1280 and set about rebuilding, fortifying the house under licence from Edward I. However, the architectural style owes more to fashion than to any real need for fortification, and Stokesay could not have resisted prolonged assault. Laurence's descendants lived at Stokesay for many years but by the nineteenth century it had fallen into decay, and was being

Stokesay Castle

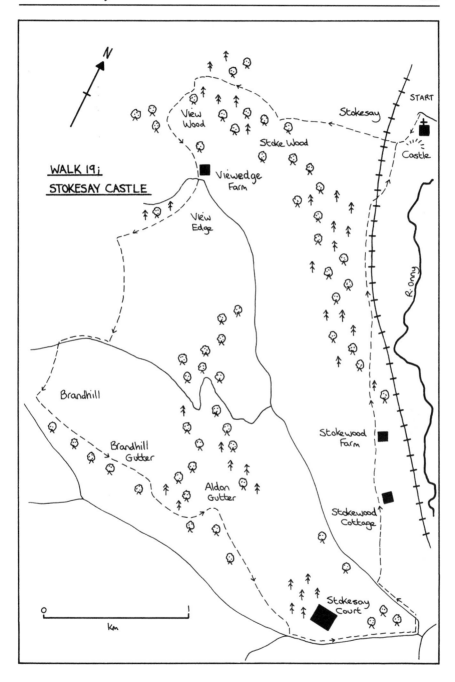

N

WALK 19;
STOKESAY CASTLE

View
Wood

Stoke Wood

Viewedge
Farm

View
Edge

Stokesay

START

Castle

R. Onny

Brandhill

Brandhill
Gutter

Aldon
Gutter

Stokewood
Farm

Stokewood
Cottage

Stokesay
Court

0

Km

used as a barn, though now in the ownership of Lord Craven. Happily, in 1869 it was sold to John Darby Allcroft, a Worcester glove manufacturer and MP, who set about restoring it. The manorhouse is now in the care of English Heritage and is open daily (except for Mondays and Tuesdays from November to March).

The adjacent church, dedicated to St John the Baptist, was largely rebuilt between 1654 and 1664, following damage in the Civil War. This makes it more important than is immediately apparent, because very few churches were built or restored during this period.

Having visited the church and castle, walk on along the lane to take the second footpath on the right, between a pond and a barn. Cross the railway and keep straight on to enter pasture. Bear very slightly right across three fields to enter Stoke Wood. Turn right, then shortly right again at a T-junction.

Reaching two stiles, climb the left-hand one and pass a cottage called Clapping Wicket then turn left towards View Wood. Turn right to walk along its outer edge. The footpath soon merges with a track which swings left into the wood for a while. Emerging from the trees again, turn left along the woodland edge, looking out for waymarkers which soon guide you back into the wood to join an old holloway. Climb to a lane which runs over the appropriately named View Edge and cross to a footpath almost opposite on the left. Follow the path along the edges of three fields until a signpost indicates a left turn at a gap in the hedge. Walk down a field to a gate then join a track which leads past a farm to a lane. Turn right for 300 metres.

Go through a gate on the left and cross three fields. At the far side of the third turn right along a holloway. Climb a stile and turn left on a bridleway through the hamlet of Brandhill. At the final house go through a gate on the right but continue in the same direction along a brackeny, partially wooded combe, Brandhill Gutter. Keep to the right of the stream. The term gutter sounds a little off-putting, but it just means a valley, and the next mile or so is one of the loveliest stretches of the walk, especially in spring.

As you approach Aldon Gutter a number of footpaths branch right off the bridleway. Ignore the first two, but join the third, just after a ruined brick cottage. Climb a stile and turn left to a junction. Go straight on to another stile and turn left. In other words, you should still be walking in the same direction with the stream on your left. The path soon enters woodland then continues through an area of rhododendrons and passes a pool to emerge into pasture. Keep straight on past more pools then skirt a barn to reach a lane.

Turn left for half a mile then at the entrance to Stokesay Court left again towards Aldon. Walk up the lane until you see the buzzard sign of the Shropshire Way on the right. Follow the waymarked route along field edges and past Stokewood Cottage to Stokewood Farm. Keep left of the farmhouse and go over a stile on the left but continue in the same direction towards Stoke Wood. Just after a gate and stile which give access to the wood fork right downhill, still on the Shropshire Way. A stile leads to a field and you bear left to join a path beside the railway. Follow the path to a railway crossing and continue along the lane to Stokesay.

Walk 20: Clungunford

Start: Clungunford, near Craven Arms. Grid reference 398787.

Summary: An enjoyable walk in mixed farmland, the highlights of which include Hopton Castle and the view from the hill above it. There are some gentle climbs but nothing strenuous. Most of the footpaths in this area currently require attention and some are badly obstructed, which means that in places lanes have to be used instead, but you will meet very little traffic. There are only a couple of stiles but you will also have to climb over at least two gates and two electric fences.

Length: 5 miles (4 miles if you start from the tea shop instead of Clungunford).

Maps: OS Landranger 137, OS Pathfinder 950.

Parking: Car park by Parish Hall in Clungunford; or you can park at the tea room if you ask first – it's at Abcott, at the junction of an unclassified road with the B4367 at grid reference 393786.

Trains: Daily service (except winter Sundays) on Swansea-Shrewsbury (Heart of Wales) line to Hoptonheath, half a mile from where the walk route crosses the B4385.

Buses: Midland Red West 736/739/740 from Ludlow and Knighton; Monday-Saturday.

The Tea Shop

The Bird on the Rock Tearoom, Clungunford.

The name may be an intriguing one but the tea room easily lives up to it. Owned by Reece and Sheila Mytton, the place is sheer delight in every way, from the unspoilt black and white exterior to the gorgeous tea room itself, complete with oak beams, quarry-flagged floor, oak settle, woodburning stove, reproduction Staffordshire china and grandfather clock. Books, magazines and tourist information leaflets are available for customers to read. It's the sort of place that's hard to leave in winter, but in summer you may prefer to eat in the equally attractive cottage garden.

This is a classic English tea room – no pastas and curries here, just a good range of teas and coffees and a selection of comforting favourites such as crumpets, muffins, teacakes, scones, soups and wonderful fruit cakes. Service is very friendly and prices more than reasonable. Dogs are welcome in the garden, but not indoors. There are plants, gifts and books for sale. And if you really can't tear yourself away, bed and breakfast is on offer too. Open: 10am-6pm daily except Christmas week. Telephone: 01588 660631.

The Walk

Clungunford stands by an old ford over the River Clun, the property of a Saxon called Gunward back in the eleventh century. Gunward's ford over the Clun became Cloune Goneford and then Clungunford, although the alternative Clungunnas was also sometimes used. It's an unremarkable village built mostly around the western arm of the B4367 which, rather confusingly, splits into two here, one branch heading south to join the B4385 at Marlow, the other heading west and south to Abcott, Hopton-heath and Knighton. Walk west along the road and you'll soon come to St Cuthbert's church, built 700 years ago but blighted by Victorian restoration. A church may have stood here in Saxon times but the present building is much later, with the nave and chancel dating from around 1300. Look on the churchyard wall for a plaque displaying the level of "THE GREAT FLOOD" of 1795. It was the little River Clun which rose to this level and a short distance along the road you cross the river and continue towards a junction where you turn right on an unclassified road. This is Abcott and the cottage on the corner is The Bird on the Rock – good news if you need a cup of tea already, but you will be passing it again on the way back. You'll notice there is a representation of a bird on a rock over the door, and it's all part of a rather complicated pun. The tea shop was actually a pub – the Rocke Arms – until 1922. The Rockes were a local family who lived at Clungunford Hall, and John Rocke created a museum of British birds during the last century.

Having passed through Abcott you'll see a railway bridge

ahead. Before you reach it go through double black gates on the left and walk forward, between barns, to join a track to the left of a fence. Walk straight on towards a row of conifers then through a gate and bear right to cross the railway. Entering an arable field, bear left to where the hedgerow changes height (or follow the left-hand field edge round). Go through a gate and straight on across a field, following the still visible line of a hedge which has been grubbed out. In the next field go diagonally right to a plank footbridge and an old gateway. Climb over into a large field and go diagonally right, cutting across the corner of the field to the hedge. Turn left beside the hedge until you come to a stile. Climb over and go straight ahead to reach a road. Cross over and climb steps in a bank then over an old iron fence into an arable field. Aim for a gap between two blocks of conifers then gradually draw nearer to the right-hand block so that you're walking along the edge of it. Go through a gate and continue to the end of the conifer plantation where you go over a fence. Ahead is a superb view, dominated by Hopton Castle below the tree-clad slopes of Hopton Hill.

Hopton Castle

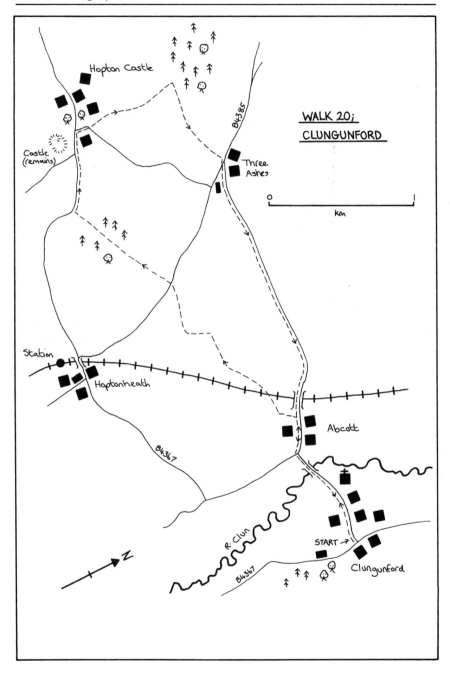

WALK 20;
CLUNGUNFORD

Walk diagonally left down the slope, heading to the left of a white house across the valley and soon joining a clear track. Turn right when you reach the road and keep straight on at a junction, the ruined keep of Hopton Castle now on your left.

The castle was built by the de Hopton family in the late eleventh century and rebuilt in the fourteenth century. During the Civil War it was held for Parliament but taken by the Royalists after a three-week siege. Most of the defending garrison were killed, and their bodies dumped in the moat.

At the next junction turn right on the lane to Twitchen and at a bend walk up a drive to pass Larkshill and join a footpath. Enter a field and bear right up a slope to a small gate below an ash tree near the top right corner of the field. Climb over the gate and go straight on to reach a track. Turn right and walk down to the road at Three Ashes and cross over to join the lane to Abcott. You should be able to return to Clungunford on rights of way but, at the time of writing, one of them is obstructed. So follow the lane, which, fortunately, is quiet and pleasant, back to the Bird on the Rock and thence to Clungunford.

Walk 21: Clun

Start: Clun Bridge, Clun. Grid reference 300807.

Summary: The walk begins with a steep climb to a height of 1295ft (394m) but once that's out of the way it's not at all strenuous, though there is another brief climb towards the end. It's a magnificent walk with fine views. The paths are easy to follow and there are no stiles.

Length: 7 miles.

Maps: OS Landranger 137, OS Pathfinders 930 and 950.

Parking: Public car park by Clun Memorial Hall.

Trains: Nearest stations are Knighton (7 miles), Broome (7 miles) and Craven Arms (9 miles).

Buses: Midland Red West 741/742/744/745/773 from Ludlow, Craven Arms and Bishop's Castle; Monday-Saturday.

The Tea Shop

Clun Bridge Tea Rooms, Clun.

Situated just to the south of the old packhorse bridge over the River Clun, right in the town centre and convenient for church and castle, this is a traditional tea room which offers a warm haven on those days when the winds blow cold over the exposed hills around Clun. Oak-beamed, cosy and friendly, it offers a very reasonably priced range of sandwiches, snacks, cakes, scones, salads and drinks. The walls are hung with paintings of local scenes, all for sale. Tourist information leaflets are available too. Vegetarians are catered for but should ask for details.

Open: 10.30am-5.30pm daily Easter-November and at weekends only November-Christmas. Telephone: 01588 640634.

The Walk

There's lots to see in Clun and a town trail leaflet published by Clun Town Trust and available locally should help visitors to

Clun Castle, built 1099 by Picot de Say

make the most of this lovely little town. And Clun is a town, though most of us might think it looks more like a village. There are two parts to it, with the original settlement based around the church just to the south of the river. This area may have been settled as early as the Bronze Age. Across the bridge is the "new town", itself 900 years old, and laid out by the Normans in a regular grid pattern which still survives. On its western edge are the ruins of their castle, built by Robert (also known as Picot) de Say in 1099. It was besieged and damaged on several occasions, once by King John in 1216, but became largely redundant after peace came to the Marches. It was probably ruinous by the Tudor period. Now owned by the Duke of Norfolk, and managed by English Heritage, it's freely accessible to visitors. Apart from the interest of the castle itself, the short climb to the top of the motte reveals views of the surrounding countryside which should tempt even the most reluctant walker.

Most visitors to the area are soon made familiar with those

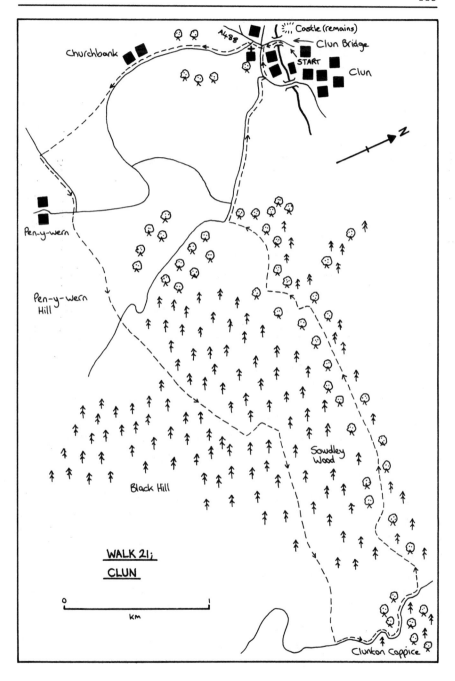

Castle (remains)

Clun Bridge

START

Clun

Churchbank

A488

Pen-y-wern

Pen-y-wern Hill

Black Hill

Sowdley Wood

WALK 21;
CLUN

0 _____ 1
km

Clunton Coppice

oft-quoted lines, supposedly by A.E. Housman – "Clunton and Clunbury, Clungunford and Clun /Are the quietest places under the sun." While Housman does use this rhyme in 'A Shropshire Lad' it's actually a traditional local saying in which the adjective could be varied at will – wickedest, for example, might have been used instead.

Begin your walk by heading up the hill from the fourteenth-century, saddleback bridge, past the tea room, to St George's Church, which is partly Norman but was restored in 1877, using much of the original stone. The sturdy, square, twelfth-century tower is characteristic of border churches and probably served as a place of refuge from raiders.

The circular churchyard is an indication that the site may have had religious significance as early as the Bronze Age. There may have been a Celtic church here, and there is known to have been an Anglo-Saxon one. Two of the yew trees are over 1000 years old. Playwright John Osborne, who lived near Clun, was buried in the churchyard after his death in 1994.

Walk through the churchyard then turn left towards Churchbank and Hobarris. Ignore all turnings until you pass The Elms, at which point you should join a bridleway by Glebe Cottage. Follow tyre tracks at first, keeping to the left of a ditch then walking along a holloway before bearing slightly right up the slope to find a gate. Go straight on to join a lane which runs across the top of Clun Hill.

Turn left, and after passing Little Pen-y-wern go straight on at a crossroads to cross the shoulder of Pen-y-wern Hill. At the next crossroads again go straight on, joining a track which climbs gently into the forest which clothes Black Hill.

You're free to explore any of the side tracks without fear of trespass, but the route described here keeps to the main track, climbing imperceptibly to a height of 1420ft (430m). The track eventually makes a left turn to reach a radio mast, after which it bends right. Soon after this it forks and it's best to go to the right, and then straight on at a crossroads a little further on.

On reaching a T-junction turn right, with a beautiful oakwood on your left, rising above an understorey of bilberries, bracken, foxgloves and thistles. On warm summer days the thistles attract masses of butterflies.

The track eventually leads out of the trees to a spot which is ideal for a picnic and commands fine views over the Clun Valley and the hills beyond. Turn left, descending to a lane, and turn left again, soon passing through Shropshire Wildlife Trust's superb Clunton Coppice reserve. This is one of the largest sessile oak coppices surviving in the county. The sessile (or durmast) oak is the dominant species in the west and Wales. It differs from the English oak of the lowlands in several ways, perhaps most obviously in that its acorns are stalkless. Oaks are not the only trees here, of course; there is a scattering of other species, such as hazel, holly, hornbeam, birch and yew. Ground cover includes ferns, woodrush, bilberry and wavy hair grass. Shropshire Wildlife Trust manages the reserve in the traditional way, coppicing some oak or hazel every year to ensure a varied structure, thus boosting its wildlife potential considerably.

Walk along the lane until you see an entrance to The Hurst Woodland on the left. Turn right, then go straight on at a junction, climbing steadily past beeches and oaks. The ground cover includes bilberries, raspberries, heather and, in July, colourful swathes of rosebay willowherb. Turn right at a junction, staying on the main track, which eventually leaves the trees to give good views of the hills. On reaching a lane turn right to descend into Clun, joining the Jack Mytton Way for these last few hundred metres of a superb walk.

Walk 22: Bishop's Castle

Start: The Square, Bishop's Castle. Grid reference 324889.

Summary: Pasture, woodland and quiet lanes set amid glorious country-side on the edge of Wales. There is one brief climb and route-finding may be difficult at this same point, but otherwise it's an undemanding walk. There are six stiles and a few gates to scramble over.

Length: 7 miles.

Maps: OS Landranger 137, OS Pathfinder 930.

Parking: Public car parks in Bishop's Castle, e.g. Station Street.

Trains: Nearest station is Craven Arms (9 miles).

Buses: Minsterley Motors 552/553 from Shrewsbury; daily. Midland Red West 744/745 from Ludlow; Friday/Saturday. Horrocks Coaches 765 from Montgomery; schooldays.

The Tea Shop

Yarborough House Coffee House and Bookshop, The Square, Bishop's Castle.

Yarborough House is near the top of High Street and is not, as proprietors Jock and Carol Wright point out, so much a tea shop as "a book shop which incidentally provides minimal refreshment". What's on offer are tea, coffee and homemade cakes, all at reasonable prices, served at a simple wooden table next to a room where 7,000 second-hand books just demand to be browsed through. Music lovers will be happy to be let loose in here too, for the Wrights carry one of the largest stocks of second-hand classical LPs and CDs in the country. In addition, there are crafts and gifts on sale, including wooden pieces made from local timber turned on the premises. Dogs are allowed as long as they are kept under control, but, owing to limitations of space, walkers in groups of six or more can not be accommodated.

Open: 10am-5.30pm daily except Monday and Wednesday. Telephone: 01588 638318.

The Walk

The documented history of Bishop's Castle begins in the late eighth century when it was part of the manor of Lydbury North, whose Saxon lord, Egwin Shakehead, gave it to the Bishop of Hereford after he had been cured of the palsy at the tomb of St Ethelbert in Hereford Cathedral. The castle was built about 1127 on a site at the top of the present town, behind Castle Hotel. What little survives can be visited from Castle Street.

The little town may have lost its castle but it retains many other reminders of its long history, with a harmonious mixture of architecturally diverse buildings. Most are simply pleasing and appropriate, but some are more notable, such as Castle Hotel, the House on Crutches, the Town Hall, the Porch House and Blunden Hall. A walk around the streets is most rewarding, and there is a useful town trail leaflet available.

Though the prevailing impression is often of a quiet, sleepy sort of place this is deceptive. There is plenty going on throughout the year, from the world's only tandem triathlon in July to a Christmas lights festival, complete with hog roast, in December. Morris dancing, a rush-bearing ceremony, a carnival and a steam fair all feature in the annual calendar of events.

Begin by walking down High Street and Church Street to the church itself, which is dedicated to St John the Baptist. A church is known to have existed on this site in 1291 but little remains from this time as St John's has undergone much rebuilding.

Turn right in front of the church. This is Kerry Lane, part of an old drove road from Montgomery to the English markets. When you come to a post box turn left onto Woodbatch Road. After about half a mile the lane bends left, and less than 100 metres further on it crosses a brook. Join a footpath on the right at this point, going through a gate and following the left-hand edges of four fields before turning right to follow a track towards Upper

Woodbatch Farm. Go through the yard and along the access track. After passing the last of the farm buildings go through a gate on the left into a field full of scrap metal, then diagonally right to the far corner. Follow a line of hawthorns then go half right over a rise to a gate ahead, at a kink in the hedge. Continue in the same direction over another field to a gate at the far side. Turn right across the next field to a gate which brings you onto a lane and also into Wales.

Turn left, noticing the remains of a motte and bailey castle, known as Bishop's Moat, on your right. This was presumably an outpost of the main fortification at Bishop's Castle (or a forerunner) and may have been built on the site of a prehistoric fort. Turn left at a junction, towards Mainstone and back into England. Branch right at the next junction and after 300 metres go through a gate on the left. Go diagonally right, passing the head of a brook to reach a fence corner, then following a line of trees so that before long you're walking below a plantation. At the end of the field climb an awkward stile to join a track along the bottom edge of

View from the path between Bishop's Moat & Mainstone

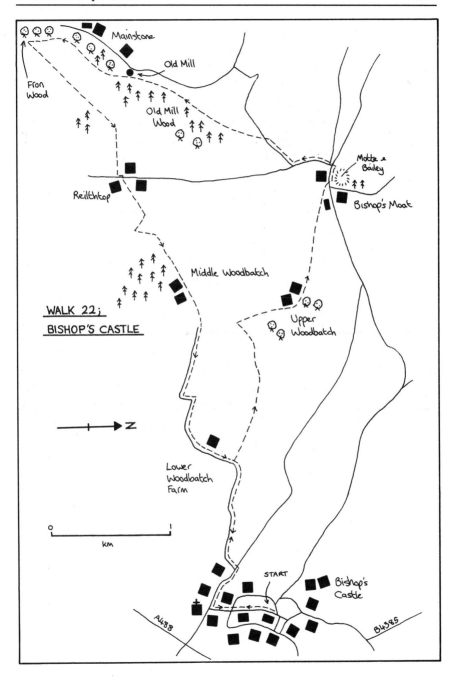

Mainstone

Old Mill

Fron Wood

Old Mill Wood

Motte & Bailey

Reilthtop

Bishop's Moat

Middle Woodbatch

WALK 22;
BISHOP'S CASTLE

Upper Woodbatch

Z

Lower Woodbatch Farm

0 ————|———————————|
km

START

Bishop's Castle

A488

B4385

the plantation. As you reach an old quarry there's a gate on the right – climb over it and follow a path across a grassy slope below the tree line and above The Old Mill, which lies just below the path.

A stile gives access to Fron Wood, where there are many paths, few of which bear much relation to the rights of way on the map. You need to climb to the top of the wood, which is on quite a steep slope, and in practice will probably choose whichever seems the easiest route. One possibility is to keep straight on until the fence on your right turns a corner. Fork left, and soon left again. Climb uphill to intercept a wide path, cross it and continue to the top. When you reach the top turn right and walk to the far end of the wood, where there's a slightly overgrown gate. Once through here you're on the Shropshire Way, which is properly maintained and waymarked. Turn left. At first, it's simply a field edge bridleway but it soon takes the form of a green lane bordered by hawthorn trees which are heavily burdened with blossom in spring and berries in autumn, making this a particularly attractive stretch of the walk. When you reach a lane at Reilthtop turn left then first right. Follow the left-hand hedge to a stile then walk down another field before turning right through a gap and shortly joining another green lane. Pass a farm and continue along a track which becomes Woodbatch Road, leading back to Bishop's Castle.

Walk 23: Church Stretton and the Long Mynd

Start: Burway Road, Church Stretton. Grid reference 453937.

Summary: The Long Mynd is probably the most popular walking area in Shropshire; despite this, it's the place to go if you want to experience one of the few areas in the Midlands which offers a touch of wilderness. This is an exhilarating but not a strenuous walk as most of the gradients are relatively gentle. It is exposed, so take warm clothes and waterproofs with you and don't attempt it in poor visibility.

Length: 10 miles

Maps: OS Landranger 137, OS Pathfinder 910.

Parking: Public car park on Easthope Road, Church Stretton.

Trains: Daily services on the Cardiff-Manchester/Liverpool line and the Swansea-Shrewsbury (Heart of Wales)line.

Buses: Midland Red 435 from Shrewsbury and Ludlow; Monday-Saturday.

The Tea Shop

The Holly Bush Café, Burway Road, Church Stretton.

The Holly Bush is a small, bright, friendly place which has been popular with walkers for years. Service is prompt and efficient and there is a good choice on offer, including grills and jacket potatoes, but the speciality here is claimed to be the "humble scone" and these are among the best you'll taste anywhere. Vegetarians are catered for but should ask for details. Open: 9am-5.30pm daily. Telephone: 01694 722541.

The Walk

The Long Mynd derives its name from *mynydd*, the Welsh word for mountain, but it's actually a large, undulating plateau deeply cut by steep-sided valleys known locally as batches or hollows. Clothed in heather, bilberries, bracken and moorland grasses, with a scattering of stunted, contorted hawthorns and the occasional holly or rowan, its 2223 hectares constitute Britain's most southerly grouse moor, while the sky above is patrolled by ravens, buzzards and kestrels. It's the largest "wilderness area" in the Midlands and most of it is common land, owned by the National Trust, so the walking possibilities are endless. There are footpaths through all of the valleys, and an ancient road, the Port Way, runs along the top of the plateau, making it very easy to devise many circular walks. Most visitors, however, congregate in the horribly spoilt Cardingmill Valley, where the National Trust apparently thinks a large car park, a café and a shop are appropriate. The walk described here avoids all this and uses several paths which are better known to residents of Church Stretton than to the bulk of visitors.

From the centre of this attractive little town it's just a short stroll through The Square or along Church Street to St Lawrence's

The Long Mynd from Little Stretton

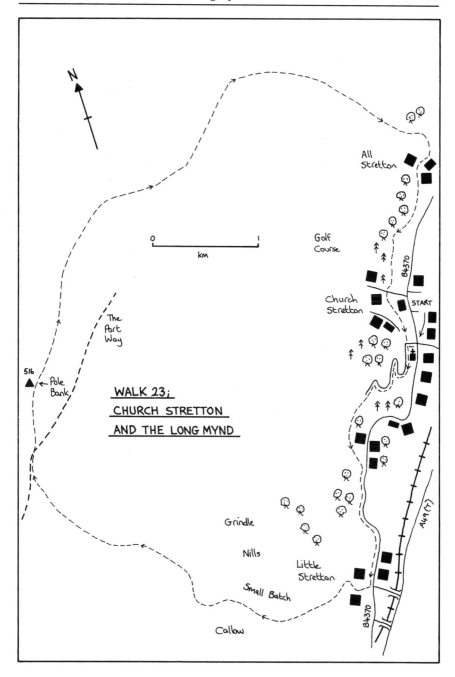

N

km

All
Stretton

Golf
Course

B4370

Church
Stretton

START

The
Port
Way

516
Pole
Bank

WALK 23;
CHURCH STRETTON
AND THE LONG MYND

A49 (T)

Grindle

Nills

Little
Stretton

Small Batch

B4370

Callow

Church. This is basically a Norman and Early English structure with later additions and alterations and it is one of only a few churches in England to be adorned with a carving of a sheila-na-gig. This is a Celtic fertility figure and you'll find it (or her) above the north door.

Continue along Church Street, passing the library and tourist information centre. When you reach a cemetery turn right on the winding Cunnery Road which eventually becomes a bridleway running through woodland. It takes its name from "coney" – the old term for a rabbit.

When the bridleway descends to Ludlow Road turn right to reach Little Stretton, which has a modern, timber-framed, thatched church, a picturesque manor house dating from around 1600 and two popular pubs. Turn right at the crossroads then right at a T-junction. After crossing a brook join a footpath signposted to Pole Cottage. The path stays quite high as it contours along the slope, below the top of Callow but well above the brook flowing through Small Batch. The hills on the other side of the batch are Nills and Grindle.

The path is stony at first but eventually becomes grassy, at which point it curves round to avoid climbing over the shoulder of Grindle at the head of the batch. It then descends to a saddle, at the lowest point of which it breaches an earthwork. This is Cross Dyke, the remains of a Bronze Age boundary marker.

The path climbs again and then forks. While you can go either way, the more direct route is to the right. Before long you'll reach the Port Way, an ancient route which has been in use for at least 4000 years. There are over 40 prehistoric tumuli beside or close to the Port Way, and the occasional stone tool has been found. It was probably a trading route, as its name indicates – port means market.

Turn right beside the Port Way and very soon the first of two paths branches off to the summit at Pole Bank. You'll probably find the second path easier but either way you can't go wrong as you're simply heading for the highest point. The summit at 1695ft

(516m) is marked by a trig point and a toposcope. Even on a cloudy day you'll see a ring of hills, including Corndon, Stiperstones, the Wrekin, the Strettons, Wenlock Edge, the Clees, the Malverns, Sugar Loaf (Abergavenny) and the Black Mountains. In good conditions Cader Idris, the Arans and Plynlimon are visible.

Leaving the summit, go straight on along an obvious path and you'll soon see a guidepost indicating that you're on the Jack Mytton Way. Go straight on at a crossroads, towards High Park. At the next junction join another bridleway signposted to High Park. You should now be walking towards the Wrekin. On your right are the Stretton Hills, with a good view of the Iron Age fort on Caer Caradoc.

When you eventually reach a fence turn right to find a guidepost indicating two bridleways. Join the right-hand one, which leads to a lane. Turn right and walk to All Stretton. Turn right by Fell End, on a lane "unsuitable for motors". At the next junction, cross over to a footpath on the right and, when this eventually forks, take the higher path. Ignore a left turn and continue to a T-junction. Turn right to join a footpath opposite a Golf Club sign. At the next junction turn left to the town centre.

Walk 24: Church Stretton and Hope Bowdler

Start: Sandford Avenue, Church Stretton. Grid reference 455937.

Summary: A fairly short walk but more demanding than most in this book, with some steady climbing (though none of it is steep) and a longish stretch (over a mile) where you're fully exposed to the elements. Probably best not attempted in poor visibility, when route-finding would be a little tricky on Hope Bowdler. There are 11 stiles. The scenery is glorious and there's the opportunity to explore a nature reserve owned by the Woodland Trust.

Length: 6 miles.

Maps: OS Landranger 137 or 138, OS Pathfinder 910.

Parking: Public car park on Easthope Road in Church Stretton.

Trains: Daily service on the Cardiff-Manchester/Liverpool line and Swansea-Shrewsbury (Heart of Wales) line.

Buses: Midland Red 435 from Shrewsbury and Ludlow; Monday - Saturday.

The Tea Shop

Acorn Wholefood Coffee Shop and Restaurant, 26 Sandford Avenue, Church Stretton.

Acorn is easily missed, being tucked away up a side passage – look between Four Seasons and Newsworld to locate it. And it's well worth locating, for it's a family-run establishment where everything, except bread, is made on the premises from fresh local supplies. There's a wide range of goodies on offer and vegetarians are catered for admirably. Substantial cooked dishes are available, as well as a tempting range of baked goods. The range of speciality teas is amazing, with everything from nettle to mango, and the emphasis is very much on healthy eating. Acorn features in many good food guides and is recommended by Egon Ronay. It's run by Chris Bland who provides not only good food but also excellent service and a welcoming atmosphere. There are magazines to read and the walls are hung with local prints and photographs.

Open: 9.30am-6pm in summer (10am-6pm on bank holidays); 9.30am-5.30pm in winter but closed Tuesdays and Wednesdays and part of November and February. Telephone: 01694 722495.

The Walk

Church Stretton became a minor spa in the nineteenth century, and such was the Victorians' enthusiasm for it that they described the town and its environs as "Little Switzerland". Naturally, the Stretton area bears no more resemblance to Switzerland than any of the other British places lumbered by the Victorians with this daft tag. And the Strettons have no need of such comparisons anyway; they have their own very individual appeal, as this walk demonstrates. Begin by walking down Sandford Avenue, crossing the railway and the A49. Turn right on Watling Street South then take the second left by a post box – Snatchfields Lane. Fork right on the Jack Mytton Way and keep straight on, soon passing Snatchfield Farm and entering pastureland. Walk up the valley, keeping to the right of a brook, and go through a gate into woodland. Stay on the bridleway, climbing steadily between Hazler Hill and Ragleth Hill to reach a lane. Leave the Jack Mytton Way here, and join a footpath opposite. Go diagonally right across a field to the far corner then turn left to follow Bull Lane towards the village of Hope Bowdler.

As you approach the main road the lane bends left and at this point you should join a footpath on the right. Cross a garden to a small wooden gate then follow the remains of a tree-lined holloway to a stile. Turn left, and left again along the lane, then right into Hope Bowdler, a small village which takes its name from one of the local words for a valley and from Baldwin, the Norman lord of the manor during the reign of Henry I.

A footpath on the right leads to St Andrew's Church, which is

Hope Bowdler Hill from Caer Caradoc

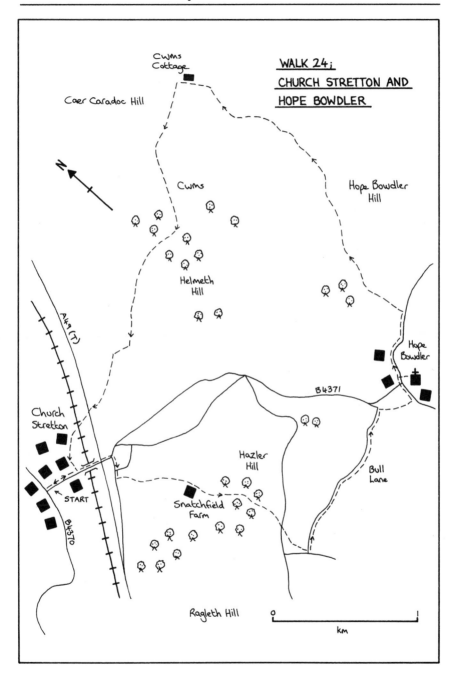

WALK 24;
CHURCH STRETTON AND
HOPE BOWDLER

worth a visit, though it is a Victorian rebuilding of 1863. It's approached through an attractive lychgate with a good example of a coffin rest. Returning to the main street, continue through the village until you see a bridleway on the left. Follow it uphill as it climbs above Hope Batch then bears right over Hope Bowdler Hill. Keep always to the main track, ignoring all turnings, and you're unlikely to go wrong. For the most part the track cuts a wide green swathe through a carpet of bracken as it swings up and eventually round to the left, passing just below the highest of the hill's three tops.

As you pass to the left of Willstone Hill (ignore a stile here) the bridleway begins to descend quite steeply into a valley, The Cwms. At the bottom pass through a gate and go forward around the right-hand side of a knoll towards a house, Cwms Cottage, by a stand of Scots pines.

The cottage stands on a track known as Cwms Road, a former drove road. It is believed that it was customary for people offering the drovers an overnight stop or refreshments to indicate this by planting two or three Scots pines, and this may well explain the presence of the trees by Cwms Cottage. Join Cwms Road, turning left and walking towards the tree-covered Helmeth Hill, a nature reserve belonging to the Woodland Trust. It's open to the public and there is a good network of footpaths, should you wish to explore. The Woodland Trust has an enlightened policy on access and welcomes the public to almost all of its reserves. Helmeth Wood is predominantly oak coppice with a scattering of other species and a rich ground flora in spring. Many species of bird inhabit the wood, including willow warbler, chiffchaff, great spotted woodpecker and pied flycatcher.

Continuing along Cwms Road, keep Helmeth Hill on your left and you'll soon emerge into pasture. Keep on in much the same direction, by a fence on the left. The old drove road has been destroyed at this point but it soon reappears, following a sunken course along a tree-hung streambed. This is the traditional right of way, but a bland alternative route has been signposted (at the other end) along the edge of the field. The choice is yours, but it would be a great pity if a historic route were to become overgrown and impassable through disuse. Either way, you will soon arrive at a lane, where you should turn left. After a short distance join a footpath on the right, turning left to walk the length of a field then climbing a stile to a green lane. Cross to another stile opposite and walk over a field to the A49. Cross with care then bear left to cross the railway and go forward until a left turn takes you back to Sandford Avenue.

Walk 25: Church Stretton and Caer Caradoc

Start: Sandford Avenue, Church Stretton. Grid reference 455937.

Summary: Caer Caradoc and The Lawley are in many ways the most shapely and seductive of all Shropshire's hills, towering enticingly above the Stretton Valley. This is one of the longest walks in the book, and one of the most strenuous, but it's well worth the effort, for no visit to Church Stretton is complete until you've looked down on it from Caer Caradoc. Take care in poor visibility, though route-finding is straightforward enough. There are only a couple of stiles.

Length: 10 miles.

Maps: OS Landranger 137 or 138, OS Pathfinder 910.

Parking: Public car park on Easthope Road in Church Stretton.

Trains: Daily service on the Cardiff-Manchester/Liverpool line and Swansea-Shrewsbury (Heart of Wales) line.

Buses: Midland Red 435 from Shrewsbury and Ludlow; Monday - Saturday.

The Tea Shop

Flinders, 3 Sandford Avenue, Church Stretton.

Flinders describes itself as a "coffee and tea shop" and also a "continental style café" and it's a successful combination. All the old favourites – scones, teacakes, crumpets, snacks on toast, sandwiches and cakes – are available, and there's a good range of speciality teas, but you can also choose from a slightly more exotic range of dishes too. A selection of vegetarian meals is always available and some of the soups are made with vegetable stock. The decor is bright and cheerful, and service is friendly. Open: 8.30am-6pm Monday-Thursday; 8.30am-11.30pm Friday/Saturday. Telephone: 01694 724644.

Caer Caradoc and The Cwms, from Helmeth Hill, Stretton Hills

The Walk

The Stretton Hills are not so well-endowed with public footpaths as they might be, but fortunately there is a longstanding tradition of concessionary access to the hills and a couple of concessionary paths are used in this walk.

Follow Sandford Avenue out of town. The avenue is a reminder of the days when the Victorians were determined to put Church Stretton firmly on the map as a desirable holiday resort. Its name commemorates the Reverend Holland Sandford, who was the prime mover behind the construction of the avenue and the planting of lime trees along it in 1886.

Cross the railway and the A49 before turning left on Watling Street North. After about 300 metres fork right, then left. After a further 300 metres you'll see an old drovers' track, Cwms Road, which shares a holloway with a brook. This is an ancient right of way, but a signpost indicates that a bland route along the edge of a field has been substituted for it. So take your pick of the two, bearing in mind that it would be sad to see yet another ancient highway become overgrown and impassable through lack of use.

The two alternative routes run parallel and eventually merge, so whichever you choose you will end up at a gate below Caer Caradoc. Go through and continue ahead on the old drove road with Helmeth Wood, a Woodland Trust property since 1986, on your right.

The wood clothes the entire mass of Helmeth Hill, the only one of the Stretton Hills to be entirely wooded, because it has always been less subject to grazing by sheep than its neighbours. Though it's mixed woodland, with ash, alder, hazel, elder, small-leaved lime and wild cherry, it is dominated by sessile oak, which has been coppiced in the past for local timber needs. The Woodland Trust, with the aid of the British Trust for Conservation Volunteers, has created a network of paths within Helmeth Wood, which is freely open to the public. It's well worth taking the opportunity to explore.

Resuming the main walk, look out for a footbridge on the left. After crossing it, continue in the same direction for a short distance, until you see a stile above you on Caer Caradoc. It's a fearsomely steep climb up but once you've achieved it the hardest part of the walk is already accomplished.

Waymarks on the stile indicate footpaths to left and right, but ignore these and go straight up, using a concessionary path to reach the top. Quite soon after passing a rock outcrop, Three Fingers Rock, you'll cross the ramparts of an Iron Age fort, and the summit, at 1514ft (459m), isn't very much further. The hillfort was the home of members of the Cornovii people, who also occupied a fort on the Wrekin. The hill takes its name from the British leader Caradoc, who led a heroic campaign against the Roman invaders. His "last stand" is a staple of primary school history lessons, but nobody knows where it took place. Just about every western hill seems to have been nominated at one time or another, and there's no more evidence to place it here than there is in favour of Shropshire's other Caer Caradoc, which is at Chapel Lawn near Knighton.

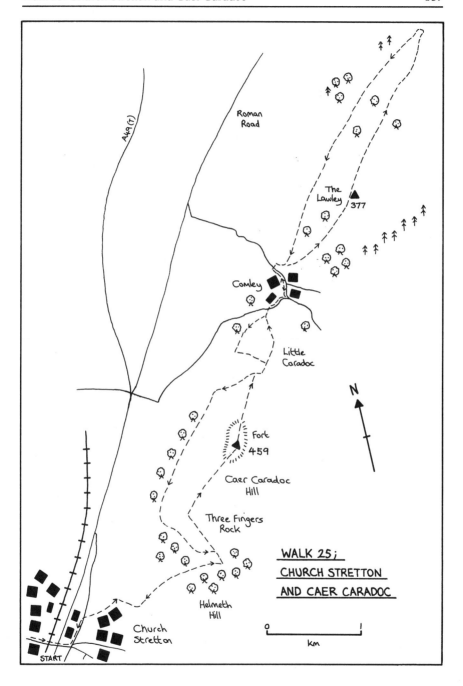

After enjoying the marvellous views, keep straight on. Pass through a northern gateway in the ramparts then descend slightly to traverse Little Caradoc and turn left when you reach a wood. Join a track, turn right through a gate and walk to a lane. Turn right, soon passing Comley Quarry, a Shropshire Wildlife Trust geological reserve. Though this is a tiny site, it is of significant interest to geologists for it was here, in the 1880s, that Professor Lapworth of Birmingham University discovered the earliest known fossils of trilobites in Britain.

Go left at two junctions. As you approach Comley Farm turn right on a bridleway, cross a cattle grid then fork right on a concessionary path which runs the length of The Lawley. It's a fairly gentle climb to the summit at 1244ft (377m). Keep going along the ridge, eventually descending to a lane where you turn left before joining a beautiful, tree-lined bridleway which runs below the western flank of The Lawley. When you reach the lane again, by Comley Farm, turn left to return to where you came down from Little Caradoc. Join a path which contours around the lower slopes of the hill.

As you approach Caer Caradoc again, a short section of the path ahead is not a right of way. Most walkers just carry on anyway – there is, after all, a tradition of access to these hills. But a detour on public footpaths is waymarked – climb up to the saddle between the Caradocs, turn right and descend past a pool to rejoin the lower path, which leads eventually to the stile below Three Fingers Rock. Retrace your steps into Church Stretton.